Systematic Training
in the Skills of
Virginia Satir

Books of Related Interest

- *Family Therapy: Ensuring Treatment Efficacy*
  Jon Carlson, Len Sperry, and Judith A. Lewis (1997)
  ISBN 0-534-16698-9

- *Family Therapy: An Overview, Fourth Edition*
  Irene Goldenberg and Herbert Goldenberg (1996)
  ISBN 0-534-25614-7

- *My Family Story: Told and Examined*
  Irene Goldenberg and Herbert Goldenberg (1996)
  ISBN 0-534-33917-4

- *Counseling Today's Families, Third Edition*
  Herbert Goldenberg and Irene Goldenberg (1998)
  ISBN 0-534-34655-3

- *Families: A Handbook of Concepts and Techniques*
  Kenneth Davis (1996)
  ISBN 0-534-25806-9

- *The Practice of Family Therapy: Key Elements Across Models*
  Suzanne Midori Hanna and Joe H. Brown (1995)
  ISBN 0-534-25098-x

- *Close Relationships: What Couple Therapists Can Learn*
  Susan S. Hendrick (1995)
  ISBN 0-534-25434-9

- *Family Therapy Basics*
  Mark Worden (1994)
  ISBN 0-534-23076-8

- *Family Therapy: Theory and Practice*
  Joseph H. Brown and Dana N. Christensen (1986)
  ISBN 0-534-05580-x

Systematic Training in the Skills of Virginia Satir

Sharon Loeschen

California State University Long Beach

Brooks/Cole Publishing Company

I(T)P® *An International Thompson Publishing Company*

Pacific Grove • Albany • Bonn • Boston • Cincinnati • Detroit • Johannesburg
London • Madrid • Melbourne • Mexico City • New York • Paris
San Francisco • Singapore • Tokyo • Toronto • Washington

Consulting Editor: *Eileen Murphy*
Editorial Assistant: *Susan Carlson*
Marketing Team: *Jean Thompson,*
   Romy Taormina, and Deanne Brown
Production Editor: *Mary Vezilich*
Permissions Editor: *Cathleen Collins*
   Morrison

Interior Design: *Sharon Kinghan*
Cover Design: *Roy R. Neuhaus*
Cover Photo: *Jackie Schwartz, Ph.D.*
Typesetting: *CompuKing*
Printing and Binding: *R.R. Donnelley & Sons,*
   Crawfordsville
Cover Printing: *Phoenix Color Corporation*

COPYRIGHT© 1998 by Brooks/Cole Publishing Company
A division of International Thomson Publishing Inc.

I⊤P The ITP logo is a registered trademark under license.

For more information, contact:

BROOKS/COLE PUBLISHING COMPANY
511 Forest Lodge Road
Pacific Grove, CA 93950
USA

International Thomson Editores
Seneca 53
Col. Polanco
11560 México, D. F., México

International Thomson Publishing Europe
Berkshire House 168-173
High Holborn
London WC1V 7AA
England

International Thomson Publishing Japan
Hirakawacho Kyowa Building, 3F
2-2-1 Hirakawacho
Chiyoda-ku, Tokyo 102
Japan

Thomas Nelson Australia
102 Dodds Street
South Melbourne, 3205
Victoria, Australia

International Thomson Publishing Asia
221 Henderson Road
#05-10 Henderson Building
Singapore 0315

Nelson Canada
1120 Birchmount Road
Scarborough, Ontario
Canada M1K 5G4

International Thomson Publishing GmbH
Königswinterer Strasse 418
53227 Bonn
Germany

Printed in the United States of America

10 9 8 7 6 5 4 3 2 1

Library of Congress Cataloging-in-Publication Data
Loeschen, Sharon.
   Systematic training in the skills of Virginia Satir / Sharon Loeschen.
      p. cm.
   Includes bibliograpical references and index.
   ISBN 0-534-23172-1 (pbk.)
   1. Psychotherapy.   2. Satir, Virginia. I. Title.
  RC480.5.L5773   1997
   616.89'14—dc21
  97-10297
                                            CIP

Various quotations scattered throughout this book were reprinted by permission of the author(s) and publisher from *The Satir Model, The New Peoplemaking, A Resource Handbook for Satir Concepts, Satir Step by Step, Conjoint Family Therapy,* by Virginia Satir. These titles are available from Science and Behavior Books, Inc., Palo Alto, California, 800/547-9982 USA.

*To the furtherance
of the teachings of
Virginia Satir*

Brief Contents

Contents

CHAPTER FIVE

The Middle Phase   66

CHAPTER SIX

The Middle Phase Continued   73

CHAPTER SEVEN

The End Phase   86

CHAPTER EIGHT

Satir's Therapeutic Process Illustrated   94

APPENDIX A

Selected Family Therapy
Outcomes: Bowen, Haley, and Satir

APPENDIX B

Family Making:
A Multifamily Therapy Research Project

APPENDIX C

Effects of the Satir Model on
African-American Family Caregivers

APPENDIX D

About the Author

Sharon Loeschen, M.S.W., L.C.S.W., is well recognized as an accomplished psychotherapist and teacher. She received the 1990 Recognition for Professional Excellence Award from Family Service of Long Beach, California. She also received the honor of being selected by Virginia Satir to be a member of AVANTA: The Virginia Satir Network.

Loeschen received her master's degree in Social Work from the University of Illinois in 1966. Since that time, she has had a wide range of experiences as a social worker in Illinois, Iowa, and southern California.

In addition to practicing as a social worker, Loeschen began teaching in 1975 in a systematic counseling skills training program at California State University, Long Beach, under the direction of Dr. Robert Cash. Since then she has taught hundreds of graduate students in effective counseling techniques for working with individuals, couples, and families.

In 1980, Loeschen received her license to practice psychotherapy as a clinical social worker and began an association with Family Service of Long Beach that continues to the present.

Preface

Students have expressed a desire to be able to more fully understand why and how Virginia Satir worked with people. This book attends to those needs, offering a conceptual framework for her work, a description of many of the skills she used, and training exercises to facilitate greater familiarity with these skills.

The book is practical and "user friendly. " It has been designed so that it can be used in a general counseling course or a family therapy course, either as the main text or as a supplement. It is my hope that the student will think of the training process as similar to that for a jazz musician where one begins by learning classical principles and scales and then improvises to create one's own style.

Satir wrote *Conjoint Family Therapy* in 1964 and became known for her contributions to the field of family therapy; however, she continued to add to her understanding of human relations. By the time I studied with her in the late 1980s, she was teaching universal principles of human interactional process and modeling skills that were applicable to working with individuals and groups, as well as families. My motivation for writing this book was to share what I learned from her in this regard. Readers may be surprised to find that Satir's therapeutic process not only deals with feelings, but also incorporates cognitive-behavioral principles, as she challenges dysfunctional beliefs and coaches people in new, more effective behaviors.

The examples in this book reflect how Satir's therapeutic process is applicable to people from all different cultures. She honored cultural differences in her work around the world and at the same time worked at the level of what she called "the universal language of feelings."

Throughout the text, the word *change* appears many times. Satir's approach is change-focused. As readers will learn, Satir would often deal with issues from a person's past, but she would do so in order to make something different happen in the present and the future. Each helping encounter was an exciting possibility for change! I hope this will be true for readers who learn from this book as well.

I would like to acknowledge the helpful comments and suggestions of the book's reviewers: Valerie Appleton of Eastern Washington University, Vincent Foley, Professor Emeritus of St. John's University, Susan S. Hendrick of the Department of Psychology at Texas Tech University, Fumiko Hosokawa of California State University—Dominguez Hills, David Lawson of the Department of Educational Psychology at Texas A & M University, Daniel B. Lee of Loyola University—Chicago, Thomas L. Millard of Montclair State University, Johanna Schwab of the Los Angeles Child Development Center, and Elizabeth Sirles of the University of Alaska.

I am most grateful to Claire Verduin and Eileen Murphy, my editors, who have been very supportive; Johanna Schwab, whose expertise and wisdom have been invaluable to me; John Banmen, who added to my conceptual framework; my students, for their feedback over the years; and most of all, to my wonderful husband, Bob, for his support throughout the writing of this book.

Sharon Loeschen

Statement from AVANTA:
The Virginia Satir Network

Avanta: The Virginia Satir Network welcomes this textbook with great enthusiasm, as it brings to the student both the spirit and the practicality of Virginia's work. It is the first book to identify over 30 specific skills that Satir used and to give examples of how each skill can be applied.

The author, Sharon Loeschen, teaches Family Systems Therapy at California State University at Long Beach, practices as a clinical social worker, is a member of our organization, Avanta, and is the author of two other books, *The Secrets of Satir* and *The Magic of Satir: Practical Skills for Therapists.*

Avanta is an international, educational organization whose mission is to support, connect, and empower people and organizations through the Satir Growth Model to respect differences, transform conflicts, develop possibilities, and enable people to take responsibility for their lives, health, work, and relationships.

If, after reading the text and experiencing the exercises, you would like information regarding further training in the Satir Growth Model, you may write to our central office at 2104 SW 152nd St. #102, Burien, WA, or phone (206) 391-7310. Avanta has affiliate training centers throughout the United States of America as well as Canada, Venezuela, Taiwan, and Australia.

Margarita Suarez, Executive Director

Systematic Training
in the Skills of
Virginia Satir

CHAPTER ONE

Satir the Person

SATIR'S CONTRIBUTIONS TO PSYCHOTHERAPY

A Pioneer in Family Therapy

A Major Influence (Past and Present)

A Visionary

SATIR IN CONTEXT

Satir's Contributions to Psychotherapy

Virginia Satir has contributed to the field of psychotherapy in many ways: as a pioneer in family therapy; as a major influence in treatment methodology; and as a visionary working for world peace, applying the principles of family systems to international relations.

A Pioneer in Family Therapy

Satir was one of the original theorists and practitioners in the 1950s to move beyond the psychoanalytic focus on the individual and look at family systems. In 1964, she published the groundbreaking text *Conjoint Family Therapy*, which is still considered by many to be one of the best introductions to the field of family therapy.

Goldenberg and Goldenberg, authors of *Family Therapy: An Overview* (1991), describe Satir as "one of the earliest and most charismatic leaders of the field" (p. 133). Nichols and Schwartz, the authors of *Family Therapy* (1995), identify Satir—along with Don Jackson, Jay Haley, Murray Bowen, and Nathan Ackerman—as one of the people who has had the "greatest influence in the first decade of the family therapy movement" (p. 34).

A Major Influence (Past and Present)

Satir was a prolific writer and frequently demonstrated her approach, modeling her work to audiences around the world. A 1970 survey conducted by the Group for the Advancement of Psychiatry asking family therapists to identify the individuals who had most influenced their work, named, in order, "Virginia Satir, Nathan Ackerman, Don Jackson, Jay Haley, and Murray Bowen" (Foley, 1974, p. 7). In 1982, a similar study was conducted to see if there had been any changes. Again, Satir ranked first, followed by Freud, Rogers, Ellis, H. S. Sullivan, Bowen, Perls, Minuchin, Haley, and Berne, in descending order (Sprenkle, Keeney, & Sutton, 1982, p. 368).

Upon her death, the magnitude of her influence and the loss to the field was conveyed in an article entitled "Remembering Virginia," printed in *The Family Networker* in 1989. Here is one section from the article:

> For many people Virginia Satir was family therapy, its great pioneer and its most compelling and charismatic practitioner. She was the very embodiment of the optimistic, can-do spirit that launched the family therapy movement. In her books, her workshops, and her innumerable demonstration interviews, she made a profound impression on the mental health field, turning the introspective, gloomy process of therapy into a celebration of people's ability to transform their lives.
>
> You didn't just go to listen to Virginia Satir present a workshop or interview a family. Even as you sat hidden in the anonymity of a large audience, she had a way of slipping past your guard and getting to you. Whether she was making you squirm by having you stare deeply into the eyes of the complete strangers sitting around you or just going on in that friendly, enor-

mously reassuring voice about the untapped potential in every person, she refused to let you remain at arm's length.

When the news came this past fall [1988] that she had died of pancreatic cancer, the reaction was immediate and very personal. It wasn't only that a well-known spokesperson for a clinical point of view or the developer of some interesting therapeutic methods had passed away. Her loss was far more palpable than that. An extraordinary presence had ceased to exist. It was as if a familiar force of nature had suddenly disappeared.

Virginia Satir influenced a vast number of people as a therapist, teacher, colleague, friend, and role model.[1]

Research that validates what clinicians have believed about the effectiveness of Satir's approach is now beginning to emerge. For example, Winter's study compared the family therapy outcomes of Bowen, Haley, and Satir (see Appendix A); Armstrong and Armstrong's study assessed the effectiveness of the Satir approach with families reunited after one member has been released from prison (see Appendix B); and Caston's study assessed the effectiveness of the Satir approach to train family caregivers (see Appendix C).

A Visionary

In her later years, Satir went beyond the family therapy field and worked to promote international peace. She wrote that she saw the world as a family of nations, and in the 1988 revision of her book *Peoplemaking*, entitled *The New Peoplemaking*, she wrote the following:

> Creating peace in the world strongly resembles making peace in the family. We are learning how to heal families and we can use those learnings to heal the world. Our global family is dysfunctional and in effect, operates with the same themes as any other dysfunctional family. In many governments, power is concentrated in one person or role. Identity is seen in terms of conformity and obedience, and autonomy is subject to someone else's approval.
>
> In and between countries, conflict is often dealt with by blame and punishment. Solutions are reached by decree, threat, force, and avoidance. Trust is frequently betrayed and therefore suspect. Relationships are based on dominance and submission.
>
> We know that the child who discovers he or she gets results by threat, force, or manipulation will likely use those methods as an adult, unless there has been an intervention. The threat used by a child might be a fist or a stick. As an adult, it might be a gun or a bomb; it will still be the same process.
>
> I wonder what would happen if suddenly during one night, all five billion persons in the world learned the essentials of congruent living:
>
> - to communicate clearly,
> - to cooperate rather than compete,
> - to empower rather than subjugate,
> - to enhance individual uniqueness rather than categorize,
> - to use authority to guide and accomplish,

[1]This article first appeared in the January/February 1989 issue of *The Family Networker* and is reprinted here with permission.

- to love, value, and respect themselves fully,
- to be personally and socially responsible,
- and to use problems as challenges and opportunities for creative solutions.

I think we would wake up in a different world, a world in which peace is possible. It is only a matter of change in consciousness. (pp. 369–370)

Through her work around the world, Satir gained international prominence. In 1986, she was selected to be a member of the International Council of Elders, a society created by the recipients of the Nobel Peace Prize. In an interview just prior to her death, Satir described her professional evolution (Kramer, 1995):

Kramer: Your original work seemed to be mostly with families, certainly *Peoplemaking* and *Conjoint Family Therapy* and then over the last years it has seemed to extend beyond working with families. I heard you say at one time that you no longer limit yourself by calling yourself a family therapist—could you talk more about this transition in your work?

Satir: Once you get a picture, a family is a group, all the things that go on in a family go on in any group. So it was easy for me to make the transition from family, where things are learned to any other group—to an institutional or work group and to see that the same things were present. So then I saw that the family was the incubator for people, but since they took what they learned into the outside world, the world became a reflection of that incubator. I began to work in groups doing families when I began reconstructions which I began at least twenty-five years ago. Whatever context I find myself, I work with process—individual, family, or groups. . . .

Kramer: Today, many people call you a healer. Could you talk just a little bit about that and how that fits in with your earlier background?

Satir: Well, you have to remember that what I say may have no truth in it at all. . . . Dysfunctional behavior comes from wounds inside—we don't have these wounds when we're born; these wounds are created and so you could say that the symptomatology is that which shows us that we have wounds. Healing is a word associated with religion. And when therapy was looked upon as something objective and, heaven only knows what else—professional—there was no room for healing. But that's what good therapy resulted in. The wounds were somehow healed and the person was able to take on things for themselves—to handle their own life . . . . so it's very clear to me and to the people around me. . . . I never did follow the idea that I was going to take a technique and push it—my total idea was "How can the wounds be healed? How can the person come to be in charge of themselves? How can they have a relationship with other people that works?"

Kramer: One last thing, Virginia. How would you like future family therapists to kind of view your work? What would you hope would happen in the family therapy field of the future?

Satir: Well, one of the hopes I have is that people will learn how to love themselves—that's the first thing and yet, we're a long way from that. And that we would learn how to grow and that we could all be teachers—I'd like to get rid of the label therapists—instead, we could all be seen as teachers of how to become more fully human. We would look at the learning model as the paradigm of change—that we could expand our abilities to see the many ways in which human beings adapt instead of comparing. (pp. 175–177)[2]

Satir in Context

Understanding the context out of which a person evolved was important to Satir, and so it seems only fitting that we look at the context from which she came.

Satir was born June 16, 1916, on a farm in Wisconsin to first-generation German parents. In an interview in 1986 with David Russell,[3] Director of Oral History Program at the University of California at Santa Barbara, Satir stated that she suspected that her grandparents left Germany because they felt disgraced; both her paternal and maternal grandmothers were of nobility, but they married peasant farmers.

Satir's father was one of thirteen children and her mother one of seven, and both had experienced severe poverty and family disharmony. Satir's memory of her paternal grandparents' relationship was that of her grandfather being mean and aggressive and her grandmother being placating; the reverse situation was true for her maternal grandparents. Satir related to Russell that she thought that in both relationships the disharmony stemmed from the grandfathers' feelings of inequality (Russell, 1986, p. 1).

Satir was the first-born child, with twin brothers and another sister and brother following closely after. She said she felt as if she had to grow up quickly because her mother had so much to do, describing herself as feeling like "the old woman in the shoe, who had so many children she didn't know what to do" (Russell, 1986, p. 7).

Satir's mother was a Christian Scientist but her father was not. According to Satir, they had horrible arguments over what appeared to be the subject of religion. She realized later on, however, that the real cause of the pain between her parents was that her father believed that her mother was more interested in religion than in him (Russell, 1986, p. 6). It was out of Satir's experience of the disharmony between her parents that she decided to become a family therapist, stating that "at five I decided to become a detective on parents!" (Russell, 1986, p.11). In spite of the pain between her parents, Satir told Russell that she knew her parents loved her very much, and that they were supportive of everything she did (Russell, 1986).

[2]Copyright © 1995 The Haworth Press, Binghamton, NY. From *Transforming the Inner and Outer Family,* by S. Z. Kramer. Reprinted with permission.

[3]Various quotations from *A Conversation with Virginia Satir,* by David E. Russell, reprinted with permission.

Satir was raised on a farm, where she developed a deep love of animals and reverence for life and the growth process. In her work *The New Peoplemaking*, she wrote, "Very early, I understood that growth was life force revealing itself, a manifestation of spirit. I looked at the tiny seeds I planted and watched them grow into big plants. Little chickens emerged from eggs and little piglets came from a sow's belly. Then I saw my brother born. I marveled" (Satir, 1988, p. 334).

When Satir was ready for high school, however, her mother moved the family off the farm and into Milwaukee because she thought Virginia could get a better education in the city. Of that experience, Satir told Russell, "In high school I had to work. I worked very hard. I remember that I would sleep about four or five hours a night during the week because I needed to get money to go to school because the need to be educated and to find knowledge was a thirst for me" (Russell, 1986, p. 10).

After high school, Satir went on to Milwaukee State Teachers College, where one of her teachers suggested that Satir seek experiences outside the classroom to enhance her education. Because Satir expressed an interest in people of different cultures, her teacher suggested the Abraham Lincoln House. Of that experience, she said, "I started out working there the second year I was in college and I stayed all the rest of the years. I did all kinds of stuff. I started a nursery school; I did a play group, I did a dramatic group with young adolescents. It was during that time that I was chairman of a whole race relations group. The Milwaukee School of Engineering and the Milwaukee State Teachers College were joined on this race relations business. So I was chairman at one point. . . . That was wonderful because I always had an abiding interest in people of different colors and people from different lands" (Russell, 1986, p. 13).

Satir spoke very highly of her college education, stating that she adopted the "Dewey" philosophy of education. Applying this philosophy to children labeled as bad, Satir stated, "the person who is in bad behavior is like a person who has a wounded wing. And we need to help that person" (Russell, 1986, p. 15).

After college, Satir began teaching, and she became very involved with the families of the children she taught. She related one of her favorite stories regarding her experiences with the families of her students: "There was a little boy who came to school and he fell asleep on the desk. I said, 'Paul, what happened?' And he said, 'Well I had to stay out all last night. My father was drunk and wouldn't let me in the house.' So I went home that night with him and I said to his father, 'Paul tells me that you were drunk last night and locked him out. You know you can't do that because he has to have his sleep. I want you to stop that.' And he did. He did" (Russell, 1986, p. 17).

It was from experiences like this that Satir decided she wanted to focus more directly helping families who were in pain, but she felt the need for more education first. She enrolled in the Master's of Social Work graduate degree program at the University of Chicago. This was the beginning of a lifelong career in helping people.

CHAPTER TWO

Satir's Conceptual Framework

AN OVERVIEW

Concept 1: The Family of Origin's Influence

Concept 2: Families as Systems

Concept 3: Low Self-Esteem

Concept 4: Resources of the Whole Person

Concept 5: The Process Approach

Concept 6: The Process of Change

The Role of the Therapist

An Overview

From what we've read about Satir so far, we can see some of the seeds of Satir's approach, such as generational influence and the impact of feeling unequal. Her conceptual framework can be summarized in the following six major concepts.

1. Our family of origin, including past generations, has a significant influence on our attitudes and behaviors.
2. Families are systems and as such seek balance; when that balance is maintained through inappropriate roles, restrictive rules, and/or unrealistic expectations, the members needs will not be met and dysfunction will occur.
3. The result of dysfunctional family systems is low self-esteem and defensive behavior, as the basic drive of human beings is to enhance self-esteem and defend against threats to it.
4. Each person contains all the resources one needs for growth and healthy functioning.
5. Growth is always possible and is most effectively facilitated by intervening at the level of "process" rather than "content."
6. The change process is universal and involves stages.

We will discuss each of these concepts in turn.

Concept 1: The Family of Origin's Influence

Our family of origin, including past generations,
has a significant influence on our attitudes and behaviors.

In *Conjoint Family Therapy* (1987), Satir describes her concept regarding the influence of the family.

> In my mind, I see the parents as children, living and growing up with their parents (who are now the grandparents), learning both implicit and explicit rules on how to approach life.
>
> I see the parents as architects of their present family. They bring together what they have learned in their own families, blending it both consciously and unconsciously to form the context of their current family. (p. 145)

In *The Satir Model* (1991), which was published after her death and was written in collaboration with John Banmen, Jane Gerber, and Maria Gomori, Satir added the following about the influence of the family.

> Our parents teach us what they know about this world, validating and not validating some of the thousand things going on around us. This is when we learn what we can expect from others, how to deal with others, what to expect of ourselves, and what others expect from us. . . .
>
> As caretakers, parents also teach their rules for behavior. Within the primary triad (mother, father, child), children learn the family rules about

safety, about their bodies, their lovability, and their ability to love. Parents expect and frequently say what and how their children should be, showing them approval for certain acts and punishing them for others. The children's identities are the outcome of this three-person learning situation. . . .

So the infant whose survival depended on others becomes the child whose identity depends on others. . . . Eventually they use the family rules as a yardstick to measure their worth; if they follow the rules, they feel more likely to receive love and esteem. Toward this end, they cultivate and crimp various aspects of their unique essence as human beings. (pp. 20–22)

Satir observed that for centuries our families have been hierarchical in nature, which has caused inequalities, power imbalances, disharmony, conformity, and the loss of a sense of uniqueness and personhood. In hierarchical systems, (1) someone dominates and believes that there is "a right way" everyone must conform to, (2) someone must be blamed if there is a problem, and (3) change is undesirable. Clearly, such systems do not leave room for individuals to be valued for their own differences of temperament, talents, interests, ideas, feelings, or needs. When this is the case, there is a loss of Self, as all the members—including the dominant ones—must give up some of their true selves to accommodate to the system.

Satir noted that in systems where relationships were such that one person dominated and the other submitted or where there was a perceived superiority of one over another, there was an imbalance of power and, consequently, there would be dysfunction. This was the case whether the relationship was malevolent or benevolent. For example, husband-wife, parent-child, therapist-client, or teacher-student relationships can be benevolent and yet can create an imbalance of power if the role of one person is considered to be of greater value than that of the other. Children enter the world in a state of physical inequality, so they are especially vulnerable to the possibility of feeling unequal in value, particularly if their parents don't know how to demonstrate respect for the children's feelings, opinions, and needs.

Hierarchical systems lack tolerance for differences and uniqueness. The members of hierarchical systems are not free to express themselves but must conform to those in authority in order to be accepted. In *Conjoint Family Therapy*, Satir called these closed systems.

Closed systems are those in which every participating member must be very cautious about what he or she says. The principal rule seems to be that everyone is supposed to have the same opinions, feelings, and desires, whether or not this is true. In closed systems, honest self-expression is impossible, and if it does occur, the expression is viewed as deviant or "sick" or "crazy" by the other members of the group or family.

Differences are treated as dangerous, a situation that results in one or more members having to figuratively "be dead to themselves" if they are to remain in the system. The limitations placed on individual growth and health in such a group is obvious, and I have found that emotional or behavioral disturbance is a certain sign that the disturbed person is a member of a closed family system. (Satir, 1983, pp. 237–238)

Hierarchical systems operate with the assumption of linear causality—that there is a single cause for each effect. In families, this often means that a child is singled out as the cause of the family's pain.

Another characteristic of hierarchical systems is resistance to change. Change is viewed as undesirable because it is perceived as threatening and capable of bringing more pain. The system operates with the belief that the way to keep safe is to keep the current order intact, entrenching and resisting change. Because change is constant in families with developing children, parents are regularly confronted with having to cope with change, and if it is feared, they may become even more controlling or rigid.

Concept 2: Families as Systems

Families are systems and as such seek balance; when that balance is maintained through inappropriate roles, restrictive rules, and/or unrealistic expectations, the members needs will not be met and dysfunction will occur.

Satir first experienced the impact of the family system and its need for balance in 1951 when she was working with a young woman who had been labeled schizophrenic. During their work together, the young woman began to improve, but when her mother was introduced into the therapy, the system fell apart, which happened once again when the father was brought into the therapy. It was only when Satir brought in the final member of the family, the son, that she began to understand the dynamics of the family. She could clearly see that the parents worshipped the son, and, as a result, the daughter was disempowered (Satir et al., 1991, pp. 1–2).

This experience was the foundation for Satir's concept that the family was a system in which the whole was greater than the sum of its parts and that the survival needs of the system could override individual members' needs. The result was the acquisition of attitudes and behaviors that were incongruent or did not fit.

In *The New Peoplemaking* (1988), Satir used the metaphor of a mobile as a way of explaining the principle of balance in family systems.

> In a mobile all the pieces, no matter what size or shape, can be grouped together in balance by shortening or lengthening their strings, rearranging the distance between pieces, or changing their weight. So it is with a family. None of the family members is identical to any other; each is different and at a different level of growth. As in a mobile, you can't arrange one member without thinking of the others. (p. 137)

Satir also observed that in dysfunctional family systems the balance is often maintained through inappropriate roles, restrictive and rigid rules, or unrealistic expectations.

Inappropriate Roles

Satir presented the concept of inappropriate and unhealthy roles in *Conjoint Family Therapy* (1983), where she described the dysfunctional family triangle as one in which the mates feel left out and lack confidence with each other. Consequently, they look to satisfy their needs through a child, forcing the child to take on roles such as "ersatz mate," "mom's ally," "dad's ally," "the messenger," or the "pacifier." The result is often symptomatic behavior in one or more of the children, who become labeled as "bad, sick or crazy ." Satir referred to them as taking the role of the "Identified Patient"—the I. P.

> In some families the same child remains the I. P. from birth, but in others the role may be shared or passed on from one child to another.
>
> a. In some families all the female children or (all the male children) will, at one time or another, become I. P.'s.
> b. In some families each child becomes an I. P. when he reaches adolescence.
> c. In some families two or more children carry on the I. P. function simultaneously. Or they take turns. Or one takes one part of the marital conflict and acts it out; another takes the other part. (pp. 37–45)

The feelings generated by the role of the I. P. can be both a sense of helplessness and omnipotence, thus the I. P. swings from grandiosity to self-abnegation. A sense of low self-esteem and worthlessness is reinforced by the parents' labeling of the behavior as "bad, different, or sick." As a result, the I. P.'s needs remain invalidated, and the I. P. distrusts others, and, paradoxically, depends on what others think.

Restrictive or Rigid Rules

Restrictive rules often govern the family; that is, overt or, more often, covert, messages are sent as to what is acceptable and not acceptable to think, feel, or do. In hierarchical families, rules such as "someone must dominate," "differences are bad," "someone must be to blame," and "change is to be resisted," are usually present. Furthermore, these covert rules are often accompanied by the rules that "it's not okay to see, hear, feel, want, ask, or comment on what you see, hear, feel or want." Satir believed that rules restricting freedom of expression are especially instrumental in decreasing self-esteem and functionality.

Satir spoke about the rules regulating the expression of anger in *Satir Step by Step.*

> Some families frown on expressing anger and view it as dangerous. Others consider the expression of anger appropriate in some situations and not others, or appropriate between some family members and not others. Finally, some families seem to be in a constant state of eruptive anger. In families who express little affection, children tend to behave angrily toward one

another, both physically and verbally. Indeed, the need for contact is so strong that if it cannot be manifested in a positive manner, it will come out distorted as anger and fighting. (Satir & Baldwin, 1983, p. 205)

Satir sometimes referred to rules as "shoulds" or "survival beliefs," meaning that we often unknowingly operate from certain rules to gain approval from our families, fearing a withdrawal of love, abandonment, or even death if the rules are broken.

Unrealistic Expectations

As with inappropriate roles and restrictive rules, Satir also noted that unrealistic expectations are part of the process used to maintain a balance in a dysfunctional system. She wrote extensively on this topic in *Conjoint Family Therapy*. Some of her major points regarding unrealistic marital expectations can be summarized as one partner expecting the other partner to:

- be a parent and meet one's unmet needs,
- repeat wounds from childhood,
- want and like the same things,
- give one a sense of esteem, value, and worth,
- complete oneself, supplying what is incomplete in an emergency,
- be the vehicle through which undesirable attitudes or behaviors can be projected and acted out. (Satir, 1983, p. 12)

In parent-child relationships, Satir's description of unrealistic expectations includes a parent expecting children to:

- make the parent feel worthy, by achieving or performing,
- want and like the same things the parent does,
- be grateful for getting what the parent didn't,
- want to do what the parent wants,
- parent the parent,
- be a diversion so that their marital conflict can be denied. (Satir, 1983, pp. 36–37)

Parents may have unrealistic expectations of their children because they aren't aware of children's developmental needs. For example, a parent may expect a child to be able to perform beyond her or his developmental capacity or may expect a child to remain at a developmental stage longer than is appropriate. A child can also be the recipient of unrealistic expectations related to a parent's projection, whereby the parent attributes traits to the child that belong to someone else and then expects that child to behave accordingly.

In summary, dysfunctionality is maintained by *unrealistic expectations*, such as those just outlined; by *restrictive rules*, such as those that restrict family members from commenting on what is occurring in a family; and by *inappropriate roles*, such as those that force a child into being the marital messenger for her or his parents.

Concept 3: Low Self-Esteem

The result of dysfunctional family systems is low self-esteem and defensive
behavior, as the basic drive of human beings is to enhance self-esteem
and defend against threats to it.

If one were to picture the impact of dysfunctional family systems on the Self, it might look like Figure 2.1. With constriction of the Self comes defensive, incongruent communication. Satir classified defensive communication into four styles, which she referred to as "survival stances": placating, blaming, being super-reasonable, and being irrelevant.

> When we placate, we disregard our own feelings of worth, hand our power to someone else, and say yes to everything. Placating masquerades as pleasing, a highly acceptable act in most cultures and families. However, placating differs from a congruent attempt to please. We placate at the expense of self-worth. Placating denies our self-respect and gives people the message that we are not important. We insist on taking the blame for things that go wrong. We take responsibility even if we have to go to exaggerated lengths to find evidence of our errors.

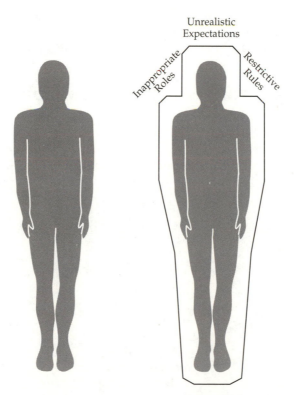

Unrealistic
Expectations

Inappropriate Roles

Restrictive Rules

Self whole, free.   Self constricted.
Access to resources. Flexible.   Unable to use resources. Rigid.

Figure 2.1   Loss of Self

Blaming is diametrically opposed to placating. The blaming stance is an incongruent way of reflecting society's rule that we should stand up for ourselves and not accept excuses, inconvenience, or abuse from anyone. We must not be "weak." To protect ourselves, we harass and accuse other people of circumstances. To blame is to discount others.

The super-reasonable pattern of communicating discounts the self and the other person. Being overly reasonable means functioning with respect to context only, most frequently at the level of data and logic. We do not allow ourselves or others to focus on feelings. This reflects society's rule that maturity means not moving, looking, touching or feeling emotions.

The fourth survival stance is being irrelevant, commonly confused with being amusing or clownish. The irrelevant pattern is the antithesis of the super-reasonable one. When people are irrelevant, they move continually. This is an attempt to distract people's attention from the issues under discussion. They keep changing their ideas and want to do myriad activities simultaneously. (Satir et al., 1991, pp. 36–49)

Satir recognized that people will vary their stances or use them in sequence. For example, a person may start by placating, then switch to blaming, and then to being super-reasonable. She noted, however, that people tend to favor one stance over the others (Satir et al., 1991, p. 52).

Goldenberg and Goldenberg (1991) summarized Satir's description of dysfunctional communication as that which is "indirect, unclear, incomplete, unclarified, inaccurate, distorted, and inappropriate" (p. 135).

Concept 4: Resources of the Whole Person

Each person contains all the resources one needs for
growth and healthy functioning.

Satir operated from the assumption that each person has all the resources she or he needs to function in a healthy manner. These resources include:

the capacity for being spiritual,
for inspiration and imagination,
for sensing and feeling,
for awareness,
for learning and changing,
for feeling,
for expressing,
for compassion,
for wholeness,
for intuition,
for being rational,
for wisdom,
for self-acceptance and the acceptance of others,
for hope,

for esteem,
for positive energy,
for making choices,
for connecting,
for loving and being loved,
for being creative and productive,
for taking charge of one's impulses, feelings, parts, and behaviors,
for being cooperative,
for admitting and correcting mistakes,
for trusting,
for understanding,
for making and carrrying out decisions,
for perspective,
for breathing and getting centered,
for asking for what one needs,
and for courage to take action.

You might visualize the Self and its resources as similar to Figure 2.2.

Satir's philosophy regarding connecting with "inner resources" is re-flected in her statement: "I am convinced that all people can grow. It is a

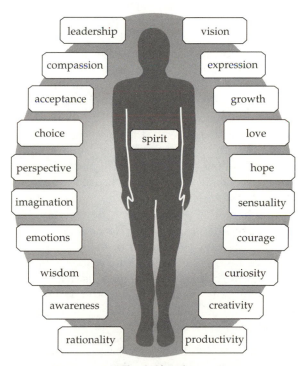

Figure 2.2 The Self and its resources

matter of connecting them with their inner resources. That is the therapeutic task." (Satir, 1983, p. 264)[16]

Concept 5: The Process Approach

Growth is always possible and
is most effectively facilitated by intervening
at the level of "process" rather than "content."

The Satir approach is sometimes referred to as a growth-directed, process model because of Satir's emphasis on the possibilities of growth for all people and her use of process to facilitate growth. She likened humans to seeds planted in a garden, in that seeds contain all the ingredients necessary for growth, but they need to be nurtured and freed from weeds in order to grow to their full capacity.

Satir taught that in order to clear the "weeds"—the dysfunctional beliefs, behaviors, and so on—therapists need to keep the therapeutic focus on the process of the client(s) rather than on the problem or content of the material being presented. "The problem is never the problem, it is the coping with the problem that is the problem," she would say.

Content refers to the subject matter, facts, details or events of a specific situation; *process* concerns the underlying patterns of the system. Simply put, content can be thought of as the "what" of a situation, and process as the "how" of the system involved. Satir believed it was imperative that everyone who is in a position of helping people grow and learn take advantage of any opportunity to deepen their understanding of the concept of process and increase their professional ability for using and staying in process as they work. She perceived process to always be the same; only the form changes in different contexts (Schwab, 1983).

Understanding Satir's process model has been greatly enhanced by Banmen, Gerber, and Gomori, co-authors of *The Satir Model*, who figured out the six universal levels of experience that Satir used for process intervention and transformation. These six levels are yearnings, expectations, perceptions, feelings, coping, and behavior. (For a more in-depth understanding of these levels of experience, see Chapter Seven of *The Satir Model*.)

Process interventions can be thought of as either internal or external. Intervening internally involves nurturing the whole person, the Self and its resources, and freeing the blocks to a person's resources, such as restrictive rules. Intervening externally means working to change people's dysfunctional behaviors and systems, such as that of the family. Figure 2.3 illustrates the therapeutic intervention possibilities.

---

[16]The specific resources of the Self of leadership, compassion, vision, and perspective were identified by Schwartz in *Internal Family Systems* (1995), a book which adds significantly to Satir's concepts regarding the nature of the Self and the systemic nature of the relationships of intrapsychic subpersonalities or parts of people.

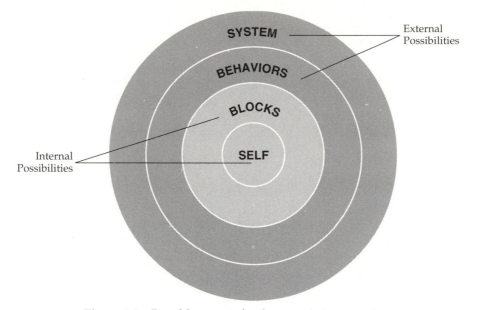

Figure 2.3   Possible entrees for therapeutic interventions

Nurturing the Self

Satir began her work at the internal level of the Self, nurturing people by validating, promoting self-acceptance, and enhancing self-esteem (see Figure 2.4).

Nurturance includes affirming people's capacities and resources, beginning with attempting to make contact with each person's spirit. In *The New Peoplemaking* (1988), Satir shared the following thoughts.

> I started a private practice over thirty-five years ago. Because I was a woman and had nonmedical training, the people who were available to me were the "rejects" of other therapists and the very "high-risk" persons, those who had been abused, were alcoholic, "psychopathic," and generally seen as untreatable. But many of those people began to blossom as the treatment proceeded. I think now that this happened because I was working to contact their spirits, loving them as I went along. The question for me was never whether they had spirits, but how I could contact them. That is what I set out to do. My means of contact was in my own congruent communication and the modeling that went with it.
>
> It was as though I saw through to the inner core of each being, seeing the shining light of the spirit trapped in a thick black cylinder of limitation and self-rejection. My effort was to enable the person to see what I saw; then, together, we could turn the dark cylinder into a large, lighted screen and build new possibilities.
>
> I consider the first step in any change is to contact the spirit. Then together we can clear the way to release the energy for going toward health. (pp. 340–341)

Internal
Interventions

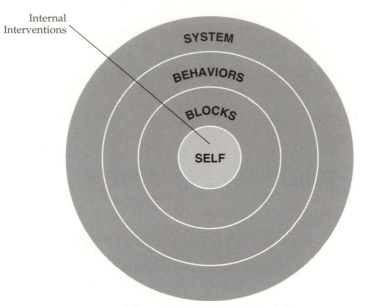

Figure 2.4   Nurturing the Self

Hope was another key resource Satir used for facilitating change. She usually began her sessions by asking people what they hoped to have happen, because she knew that it was through hope that energy would be regenerated. Similarly, breath was one of the resources Satir attempted to bring forth, frequently directing people to breathe. She believed that breath is how we access our feelings and our centers. Other resources she affirmed and called upon were people's capacity for taking risks and being courageous, for wisdom, for making choices, and for self-expression.

Satir facilitated self-expression by helping people share their feelings, expectations, beliefs, and innermost yearnings.

> The yearnings to love oneself, to love others, and to be loved by others are universal. How our yearnings were satisfied or not satisfied when we were growing up has a major effect on how we develop, mature, and deal with our feelings. In early life the Self can get so bombarded with trying experiences that it defines itself through them and limits its development. (Satir et al., 1991, p. 151)

Beyond the yearnings related to being loved and loving, Satir also worked with many others, such as those listed in Figure 2.5. Satir was always conscious of these universal yearnings and their importance. She nurtured people by responding to their yearnings, attending and listening, and trying to understand.

Freeing the Self

When a person's resources were being blocked by restrictive rules, inappropriate roles, or unrealistic expectations, Satir would intervene and try to modify these blocks, in effect, working toward cognitive restructuring (see Figure 2.6).

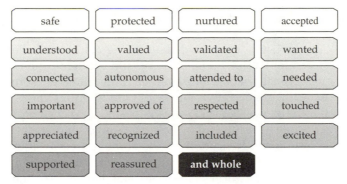

Figure 2.5 Universal yearnings

Modifying Restrictive Rules

With regard to restrictive rules, people were invited to take a look at their survival rules or beliefs, view them from a new perspective, and update them. To help people in this task, Satir used a variety of vehicles; some that engaged the left brain, and others that engaged the right brain. For example, if a woman revealed a survival rule such as, "I must always put my children first," Satir might engage the left brain by challenging her to translate her rule to a guideline with more flexibility and choice, such as, "I can choose how I want to meet the needs of my family; sometimes I can choose my children's needs, and sometimes I can choose to meet my needs." Or Satir might choose to bypass the cognitive left brain and engage the woman's

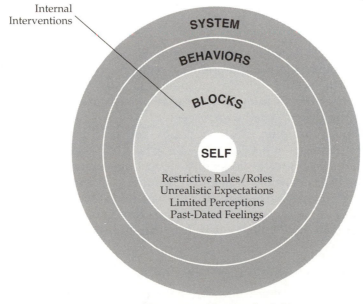

Figure 2.6 Freeing the Self

right brain by telling her a story involving another woman who always put her children first.

Satir would be listening for and challenging rules and beliefs that she knew contributed to dysfunctional thinking and behavior, such as the rules governing hierarchical systems. She countered the rule that "someone must dominate" with the concept that all people are of equal value, educating them as to the difference between roles and value. And she taught that a sense of equality can be facilitated by helping people share feelings, because all people, including children, are the same at the level of feelings.

As for the hierarchical rule that "someone is to blame," Satir educated people about the circularity of systems by speaking in terms of "family pain," rather than going along with the family's position that one person, often a child, is to blame.

With regard to the rules prohibiting members from seeing, commenting, feeling, wanting, or risking, Satir invited people to experience greater wholeness by seeing, feeling, and commenting on what they saw and felt, as well as asking for what they wanted and taking risks.

Modifying Inappropriate Roles

Offering people new possibilities for inappropriate roles, as well as for rules, was another part of Satir's process for freeing the Self. Sometimes she would challenge beliefs associated with inappropriate roles. For example, if a daughter was carrying the role of "ersatz spouse" for her father, she might challenge the daughter's belief that she "always needed to be there for her dad." Or, in a situation where a child was being scapegoated, Satir would help the parents talk with each other directly, rather than triangulating their child into their relationship.

Modifying Unrealistic Expectations

Satir challenged unrealistic or inappropriate expectations people held of their parents, their partners, their children, and even of themselves. The challenge might come in the form of a humorous or casual remark, or of serious questioning, but it was always stated with respect.

People who held onto unrealistic hopes of their parents meeting their needs would be challenged to let go of these hopes, grieve the loss, and seek new resources that had greater possibility of meeting some of their yearnings. With couples, Satir would attempt to elicit the unspoken expectations of each partner, knowing that many conflicts originated at the level of expectations. She was especially tuned into the expectations parents carry of their children, recognizing how vulnerable children are to being objects of their parents projections.

Broadening Perspectives

Satir understood that when yearnings are not met and people are carrying dysfunctional rules, roles, or expectations, they will have limited perspectives. Furthermore, she knew that people often falsely assume that their perceptions are caused by other people or events rather than their own internal process. She believed that one of a therapist's major tasks is to help people understand that their perceptions are the product of their own process, not of external events.

Satir felt so strongly about the need to help people broaden their perspectives that she created a large group process with role players called "Family Reconstruction," which would take a person back through certain episodes of their family history in order to view old perceptions in a new light and thus heal old wounds. It is beyond the scope of this text to describe this vehicle in depth; however, Nerin devotes an entire book to the process—*Family Reconstruction: A Long Day's Journey into Light* (1986).

In a more recent work, Kramer's *Transforming the Inner and Outer Family* (1995) offers new methods using imagery to accomplish similar results. He states that Satir "wanted to see her concepts applied in smaller contexts" (p. 75) and endorsed his development of new processes. Here is an excerpt in which he gives directions for working with inner sibling images.

> Close your eyes and focus on your inhale and exhale of your breath through your nose. Take a deep breath through your nose quickly and let it out through your mouth slowly (three times.) Come back to your breathing through your nose. Let a spontaneous image form of you and your siblings without your parents in the house you grew up in that you call home. Where are you? What do you and your siblings look like? How old are all of you? What are you doing? Are you together or apart? What feelings do you have toward one another? Are you friends? Do you play with each other? What do these siblings want from each other? What are they secretly needing from one another? Does anything need to change in their relationship? Let them internally talk to each other about their relationship. (p. 73)[1]

Updating Feelings

Perceptions generate our feelings, and because our perceptions are often based in the past, our feelings are often past-based as well. It was Satir's belief that, to free the Self, feelings need to be brought into the present. When this occurs, positive energy can be released and can flow. She articulated this principle in lively language, saying "our feelings give us our juice!" (Loeschen, 1991, p. 107).

An example of past-based feelings might be a situation in which a man states that he's angry with his wife because she doesn't seem to want sex as much as he does. Exploring his past, Satir might learn that his mother died when he was young, and his perception of his mother was that she abandoned him. From this experience, he had concluded that "no one will ever be there for me" and that he is "unlovable." In this case, Satir would assume that, to make a transformational change in the couple's sexual relationship, she would need to intervene in his belief system, to help him update his feelings.

Satir was especially attuned to the rules people carry about feelings. For example, a person carrying a belief that anger is not okay will feel guilty about being angry, and a person who carries a belief that fear is not okay may be embarrassed for being afraid. Anger is a feeling that is frequently past-based because it is a reactive, secondary emotion. It covers our more vulnerable feelings and yearnings.

Satir encouraged people to acknowledge, accept, own, and express their feelings. She did not stop at this point, however, as she believed that health meant being in charge of one's feelings and choosing how to deal with them.

Teaching New Behaviors

So far we have looked at how Satir worked to free up a person's resources through internal intervention. Now we will look at how she intervened externally, beginning with behavioral interventions (Figure 2.7).

Sometimes Satir suggested specific behavioral options, such as offering people new ways to communicate, especially in relation to the universal defensive styles of placating, blaming, being super-reasonable, and distracting. For example, she might ask someone who was placating to state a need to a partner; someone who was blaming might be asked to guess what his or her partner is feeling; someone who was being super-reasonable might be urged to share a feeling along with his or her thoughts; and someone who was distracting might be encouraged to share his or her observations regarding family interactions.

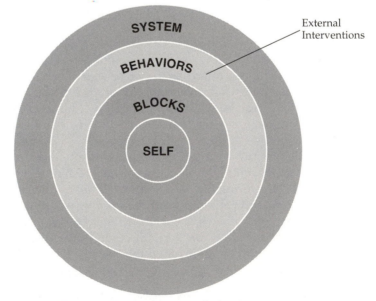

Figure 2.7   Teaching new behaviors

Many of the skills to be described later in the text will demonstrate Satir's process for facilitating new behavior with regard to communication patterns.

Changing the System

Satir intervened externally at the level of systems as well (Figure 2.8).

On occasion, Satir used experiential exercises to educate members about family systems. One type of exercise involved the use of ropes. She would attach each member to every other member by ropes and then create scenarios for the family to play out, so that they could all experience being "pulled" by the system in a physical way. For example, she might direct the mother and father to pull on their ropes, as if in an argument, until the children were being pulled and triangled by the ropes. Afterward, she would interview each member about the impact the experience had for them, working with whatever emotional material evolved. A complete description of these exercises can be found in Satir's *The New Peoplemaking* (1988).

"Sculpting" was another systemic intervention Satir used. She "sculpted" members by positioning the group in accordance with how she perceived their interactional process. She then interacted with each member about her or his experience, after which she invited them to create a new "sculpture," placing members in new preferred positions.

Satir frequently used sculpting to share her awareness of the communication stances by creating exaggerated positions for the stances (see Figure 2.9). After placing members in the stances and asking them how they felt

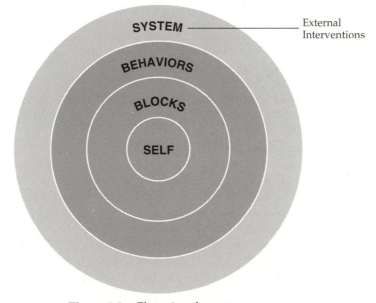

Figure 2.8 Changing the system

| Placating | Blaming | Super-Reasonable | Distracting |

Figure 2.9   Satir's sculpting stances

about these extreme positions, she would ask them to reposition themselves in a relaxed, balanced way, and then she would coach them in more congruent ways of communicating.

Concept 6: The Process of Change

The process of change is universal and involves stages.

Over the years, Satir observed how people change and concluded that there were stages to the process. She identified the first stage as "status quo;" people are aware of a need for change, but the pull to stay with the familiar is stronger than the pull to change.

Satir observed a second stage that occurs when a "foreign element" enters the system and upsets the balance. A foreign element could be a new member, a death, an arrest, a separation, a school counselor telling parents that their child has serious behavior problems, and so on. With the entrance of a foreign element, the third stage emerges, which Satir named "chaos" because people feel "in chaos," unsettled, anxious, and out of control. Satir believed that this stage offers the opportunity for making something different happen within the system.

She identified the fourth stage as "new options" because this is the time when people are most open to trying on new ways of thinking or behaving. The last stage Satir identified as "practice," wherein the "new options" need to be practiced in order to be integrated. A picture of the change process might look like Figure 2.10.

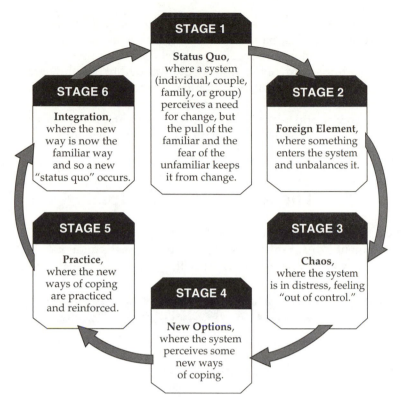

Figure 2.10   The change process

Satir consciously used the stages of change to facilitate transformational change through increased self-esteem and congruence. Increased self-esteem is reflected in a person's energy level, facial expression, skin tone, posture, spirit, attitudes, and behaviors.

Branden (1994) describes in detail some of what will be seen in the person who is experiencing greater self-esteem, starting with the physical: "eyes that are alert, bright, and lively; a face that is relaxed and (barring illness) tends to exhibit natural color and good skin vibrancy; a chin that is held naturally and in alignment with one's body, and a relaxed jaw" (p. 44). He goes on to describe self-esteem as being reflected in one's capacity for self-acceptance—that is, being able to talk with ease about both accomplishments and shortcomings and being able to give and receive affection and appreciation. Furthermore, self-esteem is reflected in an attitude of openness to new ideas and experiences, an ability to enjoy the humorous aspects of life, an ability to accept and manage feelings of insecurity and anxiety, and an ability "to preserve a quality of harmony and dignity under conditions of stress" (p. 44).[2]

[2]From *Six Pillars of Self-Esteem*, by Nathaniel Branden. Copyright © 1994 Bantam Books. Reprinted with permission.

Transformational change results in greater congruence as well. In the early part of her career, Satir defined congruence as the capacity to be in touch with one's feelings, to accept them, acknowledge them, and deal with them. As her thinking evolved, however, she added to her understanding of congruence, seeing it as a state of wholeness, inner centeredness, harmony with oneself and, ultimately, a connection with the *universal life force that creates, supports, and promotes growth in human and other natural forms*" (Satir et al., 1991, pp. 68–69). We can picture the transformational process as in Figure 2.11.

The Role of the Therapist

Satir perceived the therapist's role to be to help people realize their own creative potential. And she believed that the therapist's main tool for achieving this aim was the use of her- or himself.

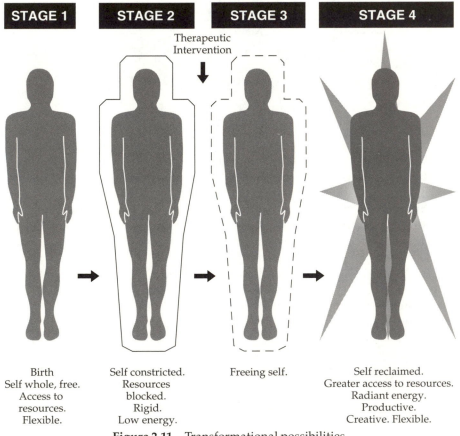

| STAGE 1 | STAGE 2 | STAGE 3 | STAGE 4 |

Therapeutic Intervention

Birth	Self constricted.	Freeing self.	Self reclaimed.
Self whole, free.	Resources		Greater access to resources.
Access to	blocked.		Radiant energy.
resources.	Rigid.		Productive.
Flexible.	Low energy.		Creative. Flexible.

Figure 2.11   Transformational possibilities

For Satir, the person of the therapist is the center point around which successful therapy revolves. She believed that when one is connected with one's Self, then one can connect more deeply with others and can create a sense of safety for being vulnerable and making changes. She stated in *Satir Step by Step*, "when I am in touch with myself, my feelings, my thoughts, with what I see and hear, I am growing toward becoming a more integrated self. I am more congruent, I am more 'whole,' and I am able to make greater contact with the other person" (Satir & Baldwin, 1983, p. 23).

One's basic beliefs about humanity and an awareness of those beliefs were key elements in being effective, according to Satir. She encouraged therapists to become aware of their beliefs so that they could make conscious choices regarding their actions as a therapist. Schwab, in *A Resource Handbook for Satir Concepts*, quotes Satir as saying, "the people-helper can only offer his or her resources, not demand they be accepted . . . your job as a therapist is to help people use their experiences for growth, and to find a way to integrate all of their experiences" (1990, p. 17). Schwab goes on to describe in outline form Satir's thoughts about the role of the therapist:

In the Area of Communication, the Therapist:

- Promotes congruent communication
- Provides alternatives and options for coping
- Presents opportunities for raising feelings of self-worth
- Encourages the participation of each person

In the Area of Enhancing Self-Esteem, the Therapist:

- Increases awareness of self and others
- Is patient and realistic
- Helps integrate past experiences and present conditions
- Makes a person-to-person connection with each individual
- Acknowledges and validates feelings
- Offers dignity, trust, and respect to each person

In the Area of the Use of Self, the Therapist:

- Models risk-taking and the freedom to comment
- Energizes people
- Creates an atmosphere for change
- Uses lightness and humor, metaphors and imagery
- Uses techniques appropriately
- Uses his or her life experiences appropriately
- Is alert to and explores survival-value situations and feelings and explores their roots and begins a reframing
- Looks for meaning and understanding, not necessarily agreement
- Has and uses knowledge of history, politics, literature, drama, psychology, biology, law, medicine, economics, sociology, physiology, and anthropology
- Has and uses knowledge of theories of family systems, communication skills, and human development
- Is open to further learning (1990, pp. 17–18)

Satir's Therapeutic Process

Introduction to the Format of this Text

The remainder of this book combines a description of the phases and skills involved in Satir's therapeutic process, along with structured homework assignments and in-class practice sessions. The homework and the structured practice sessions have been designed to build systematically upon one another in order to increase the probability of skill acquisition. A diagram outlining the phases and skills in each is presented as Figure A. In this figure, the skills are associated with a specific phase. This was done only for the purpose of clarity; in practice, Satir used the skills whenever she perceived the need.

The structured practice sessions were designed so that students can experience both growth in skill development and personal growth. In these sessions, students will take on roles as helpers and as clients. When in the role of client, students should present a real-life problem, unless specified otherwise. However, because the training is not psychotherapy, students will need to decide which issues they wish to work on with fellow students. And confidentiality needs to be honored, meaning that neither names nor problems presented in the training are shared outside the classroom.

It is also important to keep close to the suggested time limits so that as many people as possible will have an opportunity to practice. The estimated time that each practice is expected to take was based on doing it as outlined. Additional time will be needed if videotaping is used.

Overview of Satir's Therapeutic Process

Satir's overall process for effecting change corresponded directly to her concept of the stages of change. Because Satir viewed the first stage of change as "status quo," where people sense a need for change but fear it, she would begin by working to create a sense of safety, so people would have the strength to change in spite of their fears. She did this by making contact and validating.

Once Satir sensed that trust had been established, she started helping people make changes, often by first helping them become aware of their

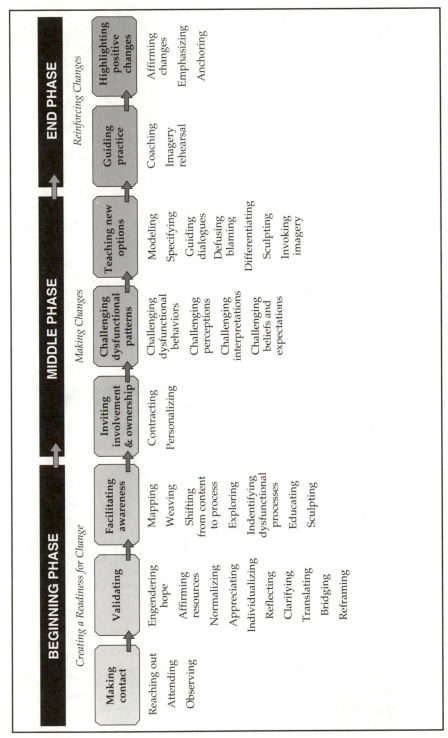

Figure A Phases of Satir's therapeutic process

dysfunctional patterns. After the dysfunctional patterns had been brought to light, Satir became the "foreign element" of stage two, challenging the dysfunctional patterns and unbalancing the system. This would bring forth "chaos," the third stage of change.

At this point, Satir was firm and strong in her support and direction, helping people work through the chaos and go forward, rather than return to the status quo out of fear. She did this by offering people new options for perceiving and behaving.

Finally, to increase the probability of a permanent change in attitude or behavior, Satir coached people in practicing their newly acquired behaviors, helping them establish a sense of familiarity with new ways of being.

Satir's process in relation to the stages of change is outlined in Figure B.

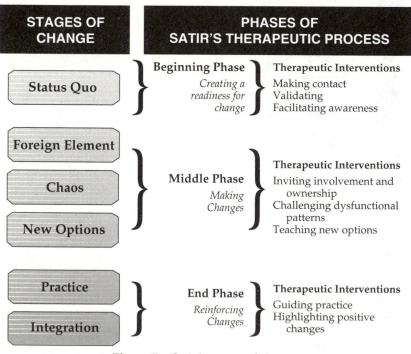

Figure B   Satir's stages of change

CHAPTER THREE

The Beginning Phase

MAKING CONTACT

Reaching Out

Attending

Observing

VALIDATING

Engendering Hope

Affirming Resources

Normalizing

Appreciating

Individualizing

Reflecting

Clarifying

Translating

Bridging

Reframing

An Overview of the Beginning Phase

As has been stated, Satir began with a conscious process of helping people feel valued and safe. She did this most importantly from her spiritual center, but she also employed skills to facilitate the process. Her skills for the beginning phase can be thought of in three categories, progressing from *making contact*, to *validating*, to *facilitating awareness*. This chapter will cover the first two categories; Chapter Four will expound on the third category. The categories and skills related to these categories are outlined in Figure 3.1

Making Contact

Satir started by making contact. Of all the abilities needed to be an effective therapist, Satir believed making contact to be the most essential. Following are some of the skills that went into her process of making contact.

Reaching Out

Satir used her mind, body, and spirit to seek a connection with people. She reached out to people physically, with her hands, eyes, facial expression, and voice tone.

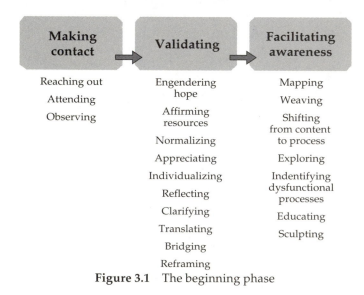

Making contact	Validating	Facilitating awareness
Reaching out	Engendering hope	Mapping
Attending	Affirming resources	Weaving
Observing	Normalizing	Shifting from content to process
	Appreciating	Exploring
	Individualizing	Indentifying dysfunctional processes
	Reflecting	Educating
	Clarifying	Sculpting
	Translating	
	Bridging	
	Reframing	

Figure 3.1   The beginning phase

She would usually begin by reaching out and offering to shake hands. Satir believed that touch is a basic human need, and so she used it as a way of connecting with people whenever possible and appropriate. Satir would also greet people warmly as she learned their names, taking her time in doing so and making it significant.

She used the position and proximity of her body to reach out. When standing, she would usually face the person squarely and within arm's length. When sitting, she would often lean in at a 45° angle.

Attending

Satir focused on people individually, giving each person special time and attention in order to make a direct connection with them. To understand them and gain rapport, she listened to them carefully, paying special attention to their voice tone and inflection, as well as to their words.[1]

Observing

Satir attended to people to make a connection with them and also to observe them. She observed body language to gain information and then checked out its meaning.[2] Specifically, she looked for changes in

- eyes
- facial expression
- facial skin tone
- rate and depth of breathing
- posture
- distance
- muscle tone.

In addition to body language, Satir silently noted each person's

- resources
- self-worth
- communication patterns
- acceptance of self and others
- covert rules
- expectations and roles
- use of power
- changes in perception or behavior.

[1] and [2] The skills of Attending and Observing were identified by Carkhuff & Anthony (1979).

PRACTICE SESSION: MAKING CONTACT

Purpose

To practice reaching out, attending, and observing.

Directions

This is to be an in-class practice session. The professor will review the steps of the exercise, and then divide the class into groups of four.

Time Needed

Approximately 20 minutes per person, 1 hour total

Steps for the Practice

1. Each group takes time to introduce its members and get to know each other before beginning the exercise.
2. The group decides who will take the following roles: helper, client, observer of the helper, and observer of the client.
3. The student-client shares a problem, preferably one that is real but not too involved, for approximately 3–5 minutes.
4. The student-helper practices making contact *nonverbally*: using only her or his energy, facial expression, and body position to connect with the student-client's feelings, while giving no verbal responses.
5. The observer of the helper writes her or his observations of the student-helper's eye contact, facial expression, and body posture and movements during the exercise.
6. The observer of the client writes her or his observations of the student-client's shifts in expression, skin tone, breathing, body position, energy level, voice tone, and feelings. (*Hint*: It is helpful for the observers to list the observation categories ahead of time and then make notes during the process.)
7. The group sits silently for a short time after the student-client has finished sharing.
8. The helper states the feelings she or he heard the client experiencing, and the client responds to the accuracy of the helper's reports.
9. The observers share their observations.
10. The students change roles, repeating the exercise until all four have had an opportunity to practice the skills of making contact.
11. The class discusses the experience of practicing making contact nonverbally.

Validating

Satir would create a sense of safety by validating people, helping them feel their value, and to be more accepting of themselves and of each other. Here are some of the skills she used to validate.*

Engendering Hope

Satir helped people regain a sense of hope in their ability to make life better for themselves.

EXAMPLES WITH INDIVIDUALS
"Although it feels pretty hopeless right now, I see new possibilities for
     you."
"I can understand why you have become discouraged, but I know there
     are other alternatives we can explore."

EXAMPLES WITH COUPLES
"I would like to hear from each of you, what do you hope to have happen
     here today?"
"I can understand that you both are feeling discouraged about your
     marriage, but I see lots of possibilities for improving the way you are
     with each other."

EXAMPLES WITH FAMILIES
"After meeting you folks today, I am sure we can work out some ways that
     this family can have more pleasure and less pain."
"I see lots of new possibilities for this family as you learn how to be with
     each other in different ways."

Affirming Resources

Believing that people had resources but that access to them was often blocked, Satir listened for evidence of resources and then affirmed them.

EXAMPLES WITH INDIVIDUALS
"Debbie, I'm aware that you used your wisdom in that interaction with
     your daughter. Are you aware of that?"
"Did you know that you had that much courage to talk this straight to
     your brother, Sheldon?"

*The examples given throughout this book have been created for teaching purposes. This means that at times the examples will be oversimplified in order to demonstrate the basic flow of the therapeutic process.

EXAMPLES WITH COUPLES

"I am aware that you both have been consciously choosing to share with each other in a new way. Wonderful!"

"As I see the changes you two are making, I am reminded once again of your capacity to change. What marvelous possibilities for your relationship."

EXAMPLES WITH FAMILIES

"Are you aware of the strength and courage you all mustered to come here today?"

"What a special experience it has been for me to have been here with you folks today as you shared with each other in such a special way, risking to come from your vulnerable place inside."

Normalizing

Satir enhanced self-esteem by letting people know that what they were experiencing was normal and human.

EXAMPLES WITH INDIVIDUALS

"Making mistakes is part of being human. Mistakes give us information for our learning and growing."

"So you see yourself as being chunky. I know something about that!" (Stated with humor.)

EXAMPLES WITH COUPLES

"You are now aware that part of you wanted to get married for security. Well, that's par for the course!"

"All couples will go through disappointment after marriage, I'm wondering how the two of you have coped with that?"

EXAMPLES WITH FAMILIES

"Does anyone else in this family, besides Keith, know about being afraid to say what they feel?"

"I think all of us growing up have had to deal with the struggle in our teen years that you are going through, Roberto."

Appreciating

Satir was explicit in her support, articulating her appreciation of people's efforts, courage, pain, and so on.

EXAMPLES WITH INDIVIDUALS

"I can really appreciate what you have had to cope with."

"I can really appreciate the courage you have had to muster."

EXAMPLES WITH COUPLES
"I can really appreciate the way the two of you have tried to resolve this."
"I can appreciate the efforts you both have put into this."

EXAMPLES WITH FAMILIES
"I can really appreciate the pain this family has been through."
"I can really appreciate the many different ways this family has tried to cope."

Individualizing

Highlighting each person's specialness was part of Satir's repertoire.

EXAMPLES WITH COUPLES
"You are each wonderful, unique people with different perspectives. I'm wondering, how do you see the situation, Margarita?"
"Carlos, what is your point of view about how the two of you make decisions?"

EXAMPLES WITH FAMILIES
"Well, Jamal, each person has his own point of view. Do you agree with your mother's?"
"Mary, George believes that a wife is responsible for seeing to it that the family runs smoothly. What is your belief?"
"Grandma, tell me your name. I know the family calls you, 'Grandma,' but I want to call you by your name."
"Hue, we've heard from everyone else as to what they would like to have happen here. What would you like?"

Reflecting

Reflecting people's feelings or points of view was one of the important skills Satir used to help people feel heard and understood.

EXAMPLES WITH INDIVIDUALS
"I hear that you feel good about the changes going on inside."
"This has turned out to be disappointing for you."

EXAMPLES WITH COUPLES
"From what you are saying, I'm hearing that you feel pain about what is happening in your marriage."
"Your perception is that you get the brunt of the responsibility in your relationship."

EXAMPLES WITH FAMILIES
"I hear that you feel discouraged that your attempts to get good things happening in your family haven't worked."
"You see your mother and father being unhappy with each other."

Clarifying

Asking for clarification of people's feelings or meanings was a skill Satir used frequently. She used clarifying to gain greater understanding for herself and also to help couples, parents and children, and other dyads, gain greater understanding of each other.

EXAMPLES WITH INDIVIDUALS
"Are you meaning that there is a voice inside that is very critical of you?"
"Is it that you feel stuck because what you have tried hasn't worked?"

EXAMPLES WITH COUPLES
"Are you saying that you want more freedom in the relationship?"
"I want to check this out. You would like more support from your partner
    on this. Is that what you are saying?"

EXAMPLES WITH FAMILIES
"Do you mean that you are worried that your son isn't saying how he
    feels?"
"Okay, now let me see if I understand this. You think that a good son is one
    who always does what he is told. Is that right?"

Translating

Satir would often go beyond the surface message being presented and state what she heard the underlying message to be.

EXAMPLES WITH INDIVIDUALS
"When you say that you are feeling stuck, are you saying that you had
    hoped to be further along in your career by now?"
"As you tell me that you are unhappy with yourself for your aggressive-
    ness, I'm wondering do you also value that part of you at times?"

EXAMPLES WITH COUPLES
"I hear you talking about your son's problem of wetting the bed and how
    you don't like the way your husband handles that. Am I also hearing
    that you are hurting about other things in your relationship with your
    husband?"
"In addition to your anger regarding the things you've talked about, is
    there also a part that feels disappointed about what is happening in
    your marriage right now?"

EXAMPLES WITH FAMILIES
"You are telling me that you are very grateful for your father's help since
    your divorce, but I get the feeling that you don't feel that he's allowing
    you to be an adult. Is anything like that happening for you?"
"When you say that your mother makes you do too many things and you
    don't get time to play football with the guys, are you saying that you
    feel like her partner rather than her child?"

Bridging

Satir was always working to promote acceptance. This could be helping a person be more accepting of themselves and their humanness, or it could be helping a person to be more accepting of another, bridging their differences.

EXAMPLES WITH INDIVIDUALS

"So, Maria, I'm hearing that you can identify with the feeling of isolation that your daughter has expressed. You had similar feelings in high school."

"As you connect with your father's determination, is that something that you know about as well?"

EXAMPLES WITH COUPLES

"So you both value time together. You simply differ on how to use that time."

"I'm hearing that there is a strong commitment on the part of each of you to this relationship."

EXAMPLE WITH A FAMILY: DIALOGUE 1

Father: Julio acts like he's not a part of our family anymore. When he's home, he's either in his room listening to music or on the phone to some girl. I don't understand why he doesn't spend time with us.

Satir: Well, let's see, Julio is seventeen. What do you remember about your interests when you were seventeen?

Father: Cars and girls.

Satir: So you know something about where he's coming from.

EXAMPLE WITH A FAMILY: DIALOGUE 2

Satir: Minh, what do you want for your son as he approaches manhood?

Father: I want him to be a responsible person who can provide for his family. That's why I get on him when he's being irresponsible around the house.

Satir: Mai, what do you want for your son as he approaches manhood?

Mother: I want him to be a good father and husband, but I don't think yelling at him for not doing his chores is the way to deal with him.

Satir: So you both want the same thing for your son but differ on how to go about helping him.

Reframing

Reframing, or turning something that was thought of negatively into something positive, was another skill Satir used to help people feel their value—to feel validated.

EXAMPLES WITH INDIVIDUALS
"You call yourself stubborn. In what areas of your life do you think your tenaciousness has helped you?"
"Would you be willing to consider that there are times when you need your dishonest part?"

EXAMPLES WITH COUPLES
"So your husband has a highly developed skill in this area." (The wife has been complaining about her husband's criticism of her.)
"I'm hearing you both know a lot about getting your needs met." (Both partners are accusing each other of being selfish.)

EXAMPLES WITH FAMILIES
"I see the members of this family as wanting good things to happen but not knowing how to make that happen." (The family was ordered to counseling because of a child who was continually truant. Satir viewed the family positively because they chose to comply with the order.)
"Joe, what are you experiencing as you see your son learning how to become a man and stand on his own two feet?" (The father had been complaining about his adolescent son's behavior.)

——————— PRACTICE HOMEWORK: ———————
VALIDATING SKILLS

Purpose

To give students the opportunity to practice discriminating between effective and ineffective responses.

Directions

This is to be a homework assignment.

Time Needed

Approximately 15 minutes

Steps for the Practice

Read the following client statement and select what you believe to be the most effective responses. Then compare your response with the answers on page 109.

CLIENT STATEMENT

"My girlfriend really hurt my feelings this weekend. We went to a party and she basically ignored me. She's been drinking way too much lately! She got drunk at a party last week and it was really embarrassing. I have confronted her but she's denying her alcoholism. It really isn't good for me because I have been sober for a year and I need to have people in my life who are supportive of that."

Choose the response that is most effective in *clarifying* the client's feeling or meaning.

1. a. "What happened at the party?"
    b. "Does this mean you are rethinking the relationship?"
2. a. "How have you kept yourself sober?"
    b. "Are you worried about her influence?"

Select the response that is most effective in *reflecting* the client's feelings or point of view.

3. a. "Do you attend AA meetings?"
    b. "You feel bad because you are beginning to realize that your girlfriend isn't good for you."
4. a. "You see your girlfriend in denial and that really is upsetting you."
    b. "It seems as though you need to get her some help."

Select the responses that seem most effective in *translating* the underlying message being conveyed by the client.

5. a. "Are you thinking that you need to terminate the relationship in order to protect your sobriety?"
    b. "I think you two really have some deep issues that need to be worked out."
6. a. "I'm hearing a fear for yourself that you will lose your sobriety if you stay with her. Is that what you are feeling?"
    b. "It appears that your girlfriend's behavior of ignoring you this weekend is probably related to her guilt."

——— PRACTICE SESSION: VALIDATING ———

Purpose

To give the students the opportunity to practice validating responses in an ongoing helping interchange.

Directions

This is to be an in-class practice session. The class will divide into groups of four.

Time Needed

Approximately 1 hour for each student-helper

Steps for the Practice

1. Each group begins by deciding who will take on the initial roles of client, helper, and observers.
2. Student-client shares a problem in an ongoing interchange with the student-helper.
3. The student-helper practices giving validating responses to the student-client as she or he shares.
4. The observer of the helper writes down the helper's responses, as close to verbatim as possible, and stops the interchange after the helper has given six responses.
5. The observer of the client writes down the client's reactions, both verbal and nonverbal, to the helper's responses.
6. The group sits silently for a minute or so after the helping interchange.
7. The observer of the helper reads each of the helper's responses aloud.
8. The observer of the client reviews each of the client's reactions to the helper's responses and states whether the response appeared to be helpful or unhelpful.
9. The student-client gives feedback to the student-helper as to the impact of the responses.
10. The students change roles.
11. The class comes together as a whole and discusses the practice experience.

CHAPTER FOUR

The Beginning Phase Continued

FACILITATING AWARENESS

Mapping

Weaving

Shifting from Content to Process

Intrapersonal Questioning
Interpersonal Questioning
Triangular Questioning
Systemic Questioning

Exploring

Exploring Feelings
Exploring Feelings about Feelings
Exploring Perceptions
Exploring Meanings (Interpretations)
Exploring Projections
Exploring Expectations
Exploring Beliefs
Exploring Yearnings

Identifying Dysfunctional Processes

Educating

Sculpting

Sculpting to Share Observations
Sculpting to Elicit Information and Feelings

SUMMARY OF THE BEGINING PHASE

Facilitating Awareness

After creating a sense of safety, Satir shifted her focus to facilitating greater awareness of strengths and dysfunctional patterns. Here are some of the skills she used to accomplish this.

Mapping

Satir would take a three-generational "family life chronology," which included the following information.

- The birth and death dates of the family members, including the dates of any miscarriages, stillbirths, or abortions
- The historical context of grandparents' and parents' childhoods, such as "The Great Depression"
- All major events, such as marriages, divorces, moves, natural disasters, and accidents
- Descriptive adjectives of each member
- The names and descriptions of people of influence to the family, but who were unrelated

When "mapping," Satir would ask for factual data first in order to increase the comfort level. Gradually, she would begin to ask more personal questions, asking about each family member's characteristics and styles of coping. In this process, she often brought to light family rules and, sometimes even family secrets. Here are some examples of questions used during mapping.

REGARDING HISTORICAL DATA
"Do you know when and where your grandfather was born? Are you aware of what life was like for him growing up? If your grandfather is deceased, do you know the circumstances of his death?"

REGARDING MAJOR EVENTS
"When were your parents married? Do you know how they met? What do you know about their courtship? What is the status of their marriage now?"

REGARDING CHARACTERISTICS
"If you were to send me to the airport to pick up your grandmother, how would I know her? Give me some adjectives that would describe her personality. How do you feel about these characteristics, positively or negatively?"

REGARDING RULES
"What would your mother have said about money?"
"How did your parents deal with conflict?"

REGARDING SECRETS

"What is your birthday?. . . I see that your parents were married less than nine months before your birth. Are you aware of the circumstances in relation to this?"

REGARDING PEOPLE OF INFLUENCE

"Were there others outside your family who were influential while you were growing up? Tell me about them."

——PRACTICE HOMEWORK: MAPPING——

Purpose

To give the students practice in the skill of mapping.

Directions

This exercise is to be a homework assignment.

Time Needed

Approximately 2 hours

Steps for the Practice

1. Create a map of your family of origin, listing in genogram form the names, birth and death dates of your parents, siblings, grandparents, as well as your aunts and uncles. Along with this data, list three adjectives for each of your parents, grandparents, and siblings.
2. After creating the family map, write a short paper discussing the following questions in relation to your family.
    a. Was it okay to see what was going on in your family?
    b. Was it okay to feel your feelings in your family of origin? Were certain feelings more acceptable than others?
    c. Was it okay to express what you thought and felt in your family?
    d. Was it okay to ask for what you wanted?
    e. Were you encouraged to take risks?
    f. What were some of the covert rules in your family?
    g. Are you aware of any roles that you took on?
    h. How would you describe your family's communication process: direct or indirect, honest or dishonest, respectful or disrespectful?
    i. What primary coping mechanism did each of your caretakers use under stress: placating, blaming, intellectualizing, or distracting?
    j. How would you say your family dealt with change?

k. How did your parents (caretakers) deal with conflict? with anger?
l. How were differences of personality, talents, and so on accepted in your family?
m. Did someone dominate? Was there a sense of equality of personhood, regardless of gender, age, or role?
n. What do you see as the strengths you have acquired as a result of your family experience?
o. What would you like to do differently from your family?

Weaving

Satir would weave back and forth between family history and current interaction in order to create a sense of safety.

EXAMPLES WITH INDIVIDUALS

"Tell me, how did your grandparents let each other know when they were unhappy? . . . And how do you let people know when you are unhappy?"

"I can see that 'getting it right' is very important to you. Was this important to one or to both of your parents?"

EXAMPLES WITH COUPLES

"We have a difference between the two of you about who is supposed to do what. Let's take a look at each of your histories and see how that came to be."

"Sithan, you seem to be in a lot of pain right now about what is going on between you and your wife. I have a hunch that we can help you with that if we do a little digging into the past. Are you willing to do that with me?"

EXAMPLES WITH FAMILIES

"I'm hearing that Dad remembers a lot of fun times when he was growing up, but Mom's family was more serious. So what does this family do for fun?"

"This family is struggling with how to deal with conflict. Since we learn how to deal with conflict from our models, let's take a look back at your models and see what we can learn."

Shifting from Content to Process

As has been discussed earlier, central to Satir's approach was shifting the focus away from problem solving and onto changing dysfunctional processes. With couples and families, this would mean shifting from the presented problem to an interactional process. With individuals, this would mean shifting to each individual's internal process.

Intrapersonal Questioning

With individuals, Satir shifted to process by asking intrapersonal questions about feelings, beliefs, expectations, and so on.

EXAMPLES

"So you are feeling scared about speaking up? How are you scaring yourself?"

"How are you talking to yourself right now that is making you feel bad about yourself?"

Interpersonal Questioning

When working with a pair—a couple or a parent and child, for example—Satir shifted to their process by asking questions regarding their manner of communicating with each other.

EXAMPLES

"You seem to feel burdened with your parenting responsibilities. How do the two of you talk about your needs?"

"You both have been sharing your disappointment over your son's truancy. I'm wondering, how have you talked with each other about your pain?"

Triangular Questioning

Often while working with a family, Satir shifted to process by asking one member to share her or his observation regarding the interaction of two other members.

EXAMPLES

"Mina, how do you see your son and husband interacting?"

"Chelsea, what happens when your parents disagree with each other?"

Systemic Questioning

Other times, Satir shifted to process by addressing the system as a whole.

EXAMPLES

"Manuel, you are feeling frustrated because Jesus doesn't seem to be motivated. Do you know what makes Jesus happy? How do people in this family find out what makes other people happy?"

"You have a different opinion on this matter than your mother does. How do people in this family disagree with each other?"

PRACTICE HOMEWORK 1:
SHIFTING TO PROCESS

Purpose

To give students practice identifying the four different methods of shifting from content to process.

Directions

This is to be a homework assignment.

Time Needed

Approximately 10 minutes

Steps for the Practice

Read each client statement, and then identify each therapeutic question following the statement, as either intrapersonal, interpersonal, triangular, or systemic. The answers can be found on pages 109–110.

1. *Client situation*: The family has come back to counseling after dropping out for a while, and the mother starts the session with the following statement.

   > "Dean is starting to do poorly in school again. When we were coming for counseling regularly, he was doing much better so I thought we didn't need to come anymore. Now I see that wasn't such a good decision. I'm overwhelmed. My mother-in-law is staying with us because she broke her hip, my husband is on the road much of the time with his new job and the kids are fighting constantly. I can't take it!"

   a. "Martha, you sound really stressed. I'm wondering what you are concluding about your life?" (intrapersonal, interpersonal, triangular, or systemic)
   b. "How are you and your husband talking about the stress you are feeling?" (intrapersonal, interpersonal, triangular, or systemic)
   c. "I'm hearing stress about the children's interaction. Tell me, how do you see your oldest daughter and son being with each other?" (intrapersonal, interpersonal, triangular, or systemic)
   d. "As you tell me about your stress, Martha, I'm wondering how the family as a whole talks about feelings when stressors come up?" (intrapersonal, interpersonal, triangular, or systemic)

2. *Client situation*: An adult daughter who is in a graduate-level marriage and family counseling program initiates counseling with her family of origin.

"Virginia, I brought my parents and sister with me for counseling because I am feeling a lot of anxiety and fatigue. My mom tells me her troubles, my dad tells me his troubles, and my sister expects me to be there for her as well. My doctor says I have to change some things or I'm going to end up with an ulcer."

a. "Rebecca, you say that your mother tells you her troubles. How would you like it to be between the two of you?" (intrapersonal, interpersonal, triangular, or systemic)

b. "I'm hearing that you feel burdened with your parents' pain, how do you experience them relating to each other?" (intrapersonal, interpersonal, triangular, or systemic)

c. "Rebecca, how is it that you have decided that it is your job to be responsible for each of your family member's feelings?" (intrapersonal, interpersonal, triangular, or systemic)

d. "I'm wondering how people in this family let each other know what they are needing?" (intrapersonal, interpersonal, triangular, or systemic)

———— PRACTICE HOMEWORK 2: ————
SHIFTING TO PROCESS

Purpose

To give students practice in discriminating between effective and ineffective questions when shifting to process.

Directions

This is to be a homework assignment.

Time Needed

Approximately 15 minutes

Steps for the Practice

Read the client statements and select the question you believe most effectively shifts the focus to process. Afterward, check the answers on page 110.

1. Client statement

"My mother is talking about selling her house and moving back to the Midwest. She is doing this to punish me for confronting her about the way she treated me as a child. I don't want her to go. She's too old to be moving away. How can I stop her?"

a. "Where does she want to move to?"

    b. "What do you feel as you think about your mother moving?"

2. Client statement

"My husband is driving me crazy. He cleans up everything immediately. I can't even leave a cup of coffee sitting around because he will come and get it and wash it up. We've only been married a month, and already I want to leave him. I can't see myself living with someone this compulsive for the rest of my life!"

    a. "How have the two of you dealt with other differences?"
    b. "What other ways does he aggravate you?"

3. Client statement

"My children are out of control. They speak very disrespectfully to me. They don't listen to me. They are getting worse and worse. What should I do?"

    a. "What do you mean by disrespectful?"
    b. "How did people show respect in your family when you were growing up?"

——————— PRACTICE HOMEWORK 3: ———————
 SHIFTING TO PROCESS

Purpose

To give students the opportunity to practice shifting to process by writing questions.

Directions

This is to be a homework assignment.

Time Needed

Approximately 1 hour

Steps for the Practice

After reading the client statements, write a reflective response to the client, followed by a question shifting the focus to process. The professor will then evaluate your responses and questions. Here is an example.

CLIENT STATEMENT

"I don't know what to do. I need your help to decide whether to follow through on my decision to take my daughter to a speech therapist. My husband doesn't think that she needs to go. I get so frightened when he disagrees with me. Maybe I'll take her secretly and not tell him and wait to see what the therapist has to say. What do you think; should I take her or not?"

REFLECTIVE RESPONSE

"You sound really torn because you want to meet your daughter's needs, but you also don't want to upset your husband."

PROCESS QUESTION

"What are you saying to yourself about his reaction that is creating your fear?"

1. Client statement

"I need some advice and help. I have taken in my elderly parents because my father is senile and my mother can't handle him by herself. They brought three cats and a dog and I'm allergic to them. They have lost so much that I find it hard to insist that they get rid of their animals, but I am really suffering. It has me so depressed that I'm not functioning very well. I can't concentrate at work and I just hide out in my bedroom at night. What do you suggest I do?"

a. Write a reflective response.
b. Write a process question.

2. Client statement

"My husband and I had a big quarrel last night. I had spent hours preparing a very special meal and I expected him home at 6 P.M., as we had agreed. He showed up at 7 P.M. and had totally forgotten that we were having a special meal. These things don't matter to him. He would have been happy with hot dogs! Don't you think he should have remembered?"

a. Write a reflective response.
b. Write a process question.

3. Client statement

"Our kids fight all the time. Kenny teases Suzy until she starts crying, then my wife screams at Kenny. Every night, this is what I have to listen to and I'm sick of it. I tell my wife to get stricter with Kenny but she gets mad at me."

a. Write a reflective response.
b. Write a process question.

————— PRACTICE SESSION: ————— SHIFTING TO PROCESS

Purpose

To give students the opportunity to practice shifting from the problem to the process in a simulated family counseling situation.

Directions

This is to be an in-class practice session. The class will divide into groups of six or seven for a family counseling role play.

Time Needed

Approximately 1 hour per role play

Steps for the Practice

1. The students decide who will take on the roles of helper, observer, and family members.
2. The family role players separate from the helper and observer and decide on a presenting problem.
3. The helper conducts a mock counseling session for approximately 30 minutes, practicing shifting the focus off the problem and onto the role-play family's process.
4. The observer writes down each question the helper uses to attempt to shift to process.
5. When the role play has ended, the observer reads the helper's questions and the group evaluates its effectiveness.
6. The class reconvenes and discusses the experience.

Exploring

To this point, the skills of mapping, weaving, and shifting from content to process have been described as ways in which Satir worked to facilitate awareness. The next skill to be described is that of exploring.

Satir explored for feelings: feelings about feelings, perceptions, meanings, projections, beliefs and rules, expectations, and yearnings. She was searching for the blocks or constraints to the Self that could be lifted, such as past-dated feelings, limited perceptions, restrictive rules or unhelpful beliefs, inappropriate expectations, and unfulfilled yearnings.

To aid in the conceptualization of the levels of experience Satir used for exploring and intervention, Banmen, Gerber, and Gomori (Satir et al., 1991) present a metaphor they call the "personal iceberg." The tip of the iceberg represents that which is visible, behavior and coping; feelings, perceptions, expectations, and yearnings are below the surface and overlay the Self.

Another metaphorical aid that can be helpful is to think of a musical scale, with the note below the staff representing our innermost yearnings; the note above the staff representing that which is visible, our behaviors; and the notes in between representing areas that influence our behaviors, such as feelings, perceptions, meanings, expectations, beliefs, and yearnings. Visually, the progression might resemble Figure 4.1.

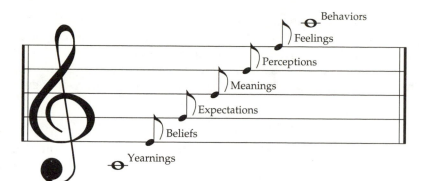

Figure 4.1   Levels of the Self

Exploring Feelings

Believing that feelings are the source of energy, Satir frequently explored for feelings.

EXAMPLES WITH INDIVIDUALS
"What are you feeling at this moment?"
"Go inside and tell me what you are feeling."

EXAMPLES WITH COUPLES
"What are you feeling as you hear your husband talk about his pain?"
"As you get in touch with the expectations carried into the marriage, how are you feeling?"

EXAMPLES WITH FAMILIES
"Now that you are aware of this new picture of your father, what are you feeling?"
"How do you feel as you watch your husband and son share with each other?"

Exploring Feelings about Feelings

Satir explored not only for feelings but also for feelings about feelings! As a result, she frequently was able to uncover family rules.

EXAMPLES WITH INDIVIDUALS
"How do you feel about feeling angry with your father?"
"Being aware that you are relieved that your mother isn't able to come for a visit, how do you feel about feeling relieved?"

EXAMPLES WITH COUPLES
"As you get in touch with your disappointment about the relationship, how do you feel?"
"How does it feel to feel closer to your partner?"

EXAMPLES WITH FAMILIES

"Being aware of the sadness you feel about the distance between you and
your son Jesse, how do you feel about feeling sad, John?"

"I see this family being proud of the steps you have taken today to connect
more fully with each other. And I'm just wondering, how does that
feel?"

Exploring Perceptions

Recognizing that feelings are based on perceptions, Satir would often begin
exploring for what the client is seeing and hearing.

EXAMPLES WITH INDIVIDUALS

"What are you seeing that you are reacting to?"

"What are you hearing me say to you?"

EXAMPLES WITH COUPLES

"As you listen to your partner, what are you hearing going on with him?"

"What do you see as you look at his expression?"

EXAMPLES WITH FAMILIES

"As your son speaks to you, what are you hearing him say?"

"What are you seeing as you watch your daughter and son talk with each
other?"

Exploring Meanings (Interpretations)

In addition to exploring for what a person was seeing or hearing, Satir would
explore for the meaning being given to what was being seen or heard.

EXAMPLES WITH INDIVIDUALS

"What meaning are you giving to this situation that is causing you to feel
bad?"

"How are you interpreting this situation to mean that you don't fit in?"

EXAMPLES WITH COUPLES

"As you look at your husband's face, what meaning do you give to what
you see?"

"How do you interpret your wife's statement that she needs more of your
time?"

EXAMPLES WITH FAMILIES

"When your mother says she wants the family to be closer, what does that
mean to you? How do you interpret that?"

"I'm aware that you have been listening intently to your father. How do
you interpret what you are hearing?"

Exploring Projections

Satir often took her exploration of meanings beyond the examples just described when she suspected that they were based on projections.

EXAMPLE WITH A COUPLE

Satir: As you hear your husband's voice, what is happening for you, Yoko?

Yoko: I'm feeling very frightened.

Satir: What is frightening you?

Yoko: He sounds angry with me.

Satir: How does that frighten you?

Yoko: I guess I'm afraid he's going to hurt me.

Satir: Has he ever done that?

Yoko: No.

Satir: What do you think the fear is about then?

Yoko: Well, when I was little and my father got angry with my mother, he would sometimes hit her.

Satir: So you have carried that fear over to your husband.

Yoko: Yes, I guess I have.

EXAMPLE OF EXPLORING PROJECTIONS WITH A FAMILY

Diana: Rick defies me all of the time! He and his father are just alike.

Satir: When your son says "no" to you, do you see him as being like his father?

Diana: Yes, they are both stubborn.

Satir: How do you experience your husband as being stubborn?

Diana: Well, when he gets something in his head, he won't change his mind.

Satir: That's frustrating for you.

Diana: Yes, very.

Satir: Are there times when Rick is cooperative as well?

Diana: Yes.

Satir: We all put feelings on people that don't belong to them from time to time. I'm wondering if your feeling of frustration has more to do with your relationship with your husband than with Rick.

Diana: That's a possibility.

Exploring Expectations

Another significant area for exploration for Satir was that of expectations. Expectations could be of oneself or of another.

EXAMPLES WITH INDIVIDUALS

"What did you expect of yourself in relation to getting angry?"
"Do you expect yourself to do it perfectly every time?"

EXAMPLES WITH COUPLES

"What were your expectations for a husband, Jean?"

"James, as you think back to before you were married, what did you
    expect your wife would be like."

EXAMPLES WITH FAMILIES

"Oscar, when you were told that you were going to be the father of a little
    girl, what did you expect that would be like?"

"Noemi, what did you expect life would be like coming into a ready-made
    family?"

Exploring Beliefs

Satir often explored for the beliefs underlying unhealthy expectations.

EXAMPLES WITH INDIVIDUALS

"It sounds as if you believe it's dangerous to ask for what you want. Is that
    so?"

"Do you believe you have a choice in this situation?"

EXAMPLES WITH COUPLES

"I hear you believing that your wife doesn't love you if she differs with
    you on this. Is that what you are saying to yourself?"

"Is it your belief that your husband should know how you want to be
    cared for without your having to tell him?"

EXAMPLES WITH FAMILIES

"Isabel, what do you believe will happen if you share your feelings with
    your mother?"

"Maulana, as you express concern regarding your son's adventurous
    nature, I'm wondering, do you believe the world is a dangerous
    place?"

In addition to direct exploration for the beliefs (rules) of a family, Satir
also explored for them indirectly. She did this by asking how the family dealt
with critical areas, such as angry feelings and disagreements.

"I'm wondering, how do people in this family let each other know when
    they are angry?"

"Janice, what happens in this family when people don't agree?"

Exploring Yearnings

Going even deeper than beliefs, Satir would explore for the underlying yearnings.

EXAMPLES WITH INDIVIDUALS

"You feel angry with your mother because she repeatedly disappoints you.
    What is it that you long for from your mother?"

"You look pained as you talk about feeling your father's disapproval of
    you. Is there a yearning inside for his approval?"

EXAMPLES WITH COUPLES

"Yoeng, as you experience the feeling of being abandoned by your husband, are you aware of any longing as a child for your father to be there for you?"

"Toek, as you express your disappointment at not being recognized for your talents and efforts in your marriage, I'm wondering, has there been a yearning within you for recognition that began even before you were married?"

EXAMPLES WITH FAMILIES

"Dana, as I hear you sharing here with your family about your mother and the children's grandmother, I have the strong sense that you long for her acceptance. Does that fit at all?"

"As you hear your son expressing a desire to have more of your undivided attention, does this feel familiar? Was this something you longed for from your father?"

———————— PRACTICE————————
HOMEWORK 1: EXPLORING

Purpose

To give students practice in identifying dysfunctional beliefs.

Directions

This is to be a homework assignment.

Time Needed

Approximately 30 minutes

Steps for the Practice

1. Read each of the client-helper dialogues given below and write out possible underlying beliefs of the clients.
2. Compare your ideas regarding the client's beliefs with those in the answers on pages 110 to 111.

Client-Helper Dialogues

1. A female client is talking with a helper about her fear of losing a friend.

    Client: I'm really upset. Now that I have been promoted to a position of authority in my job, my co-worker, whom I have thought of as a friend as well as a co-worker, is acting distant toward me.

Helper: You feel bad because you've lost some special closeness with your friend.

Client: Yes, we have been really close. I think of her as my best friend. And then I start thinking about all of the other people who are not returning my calls. I get the feeling that people are purposefully distancing themselves from me.

Helper: You are worried that it's more than accidental that you aren't hearing from friends.

Client: I keep wondering what there is about me that people don't like. My mother always told me that I was not likable, that I would never be able to have friends. And it appears that she was right; there is something basically wrong with me.

a.   List some of the client's possible beliefs.

2. A male client is talking with a helper regarding his sense of insecurity.

Client: The leader of my Kiwanis Club asked me if I would take on an additional project, and I told him I was too busy right now and that I couldn't do it. I felt good about setting some limits and taking care of myself, but the more I thought about it, the more I have worried about how easily he accepted my rejection of his request.

Helper: What worried you about that?

Client: Well, maybe he really doesn't like me. Maybe the men are just pretending to value my leadership. Maybe they really don't want me.

Helper: Are you worried that they aren't being honest with you?

Client: Yeah. I've always been an outsider when it comes to groups. I've never really belonged. I always think people are not going to accept me. I think they are going to throw me away.

a.   List some of the client's possible beliefs.

3. A male client is talking with a helper about his rage toward his wife.

Client: I know that I am in trouble for hitting my wife again, but I can't seem to stop. I promise myself that I won't do it again and it's okay for several months. In fact, there are times when I have gone for two or three years, and then she does something that just infuriates me so much that I end up hitting her again.

Helper: You find yourself unable to control your anger with her.

Client: Yeah. She frustrates me beyond belief. I can't make her
      understand.

Helper: What is it that you want her to understand?

Client: How upset I get about the money. I work hard and she
      never appreciates it. I have even taken second jobs, but she
      doesn't care. All she cares about is what she doesn't have.
      There is no way to satisfy this woman. All women want is to be
      taken care of.

Helper: Do you feel hurt by her lack of appreciation?

Client: Yes. She should appreciate my efforts and I see no evi-
      dence of that.

  a. List some of the client's possible beliefs.

4. A female client is talking with a helper about her pain over her
    recent separation from her husband.

Client: My husband has separated from me. He's sleeping at his
      office. I've pleaded with him to come home, but he won't.

Helper: Are you frightened?

Client: Yes. I don't want to be alone. We've been married for 20
      years, and he's the only man I trust. As far as I know, he's not
      involved with anyone else. Why won't he come home? I've
      stopped drinking and that is what he was complaining about,
      so why won't he come back home?

Helper: You can't understand what's going on with him.

Client: He won't talk. I went to his office yesterday, but he
      wouldn't talk with me. When I asked him what he was think-
      ing, he said that his mind was a blank.

Helper: You don't know how to find out what's going on with
      him.

Client: He's always been a quiet man. I've carried much of the
      load for the family. There have been many years that he didn't
      even work. I have always worked outside the home, done the
      bills, kept the house, and taken care of the children. My mother
      used to see me so tired all the time and tell me that I should get
      him to help me. I just couldn't.

Helper: It was too hard to ask for his help.

Client: I guess so. I guess I was afraid he'd leave me if I asked for
      his help. I don't see myself as any great prize. Other people tell
      me he's not worth it, but I don't see it that way. I want him
      back, no matter what.

  a.   List some of the client's possible beliefs.

————PRACTICE————
HOMEWORK 2: EXPLORING

Purpose

To give students greater familiarity with possible areas for exploration by using the musical scale model.

Directions

This is to be a homework assignment.

Time Needed

Approximately 30 minutes

Steps for the Practice

Write down a behavior that you would like to change and then work down the scale exploring within yourself. Here is an example to follow.

1. What **behavior** do I wish to change?

   "I would like to stop saying unkind things to my husband when I discover that he hasn't done the dishes while I was at school."

2. What **feelings** do I experience regarding this situation?

   "I feel angry."

3. What am I **perceiving** (seeing and/or hearing)?

   "I see dirty dishes."

4. What **meaning** am I giving to what I am perceiving?

   "He doesn't care about my feelings."

5. What **expectation(s)** am I holding that are influencing my feelings?

   "He should know how hard I am working in school and help out."

6. What **belief(s)** am I holding that are influencing my feelings?

   "Men will take advantage of women and if he really loved me, he would see what needed to be done and do it."

7. What am I **yearning** for?

   "I am yearning for acknowledgment."

8. Upon reexamination of my expectations and beliefs, I would like to make these changes.

   "I would like to stop making negative generalizations about men. Instead, I would like to stick to the issue at hand and ask for help in a nonreactive manner."

——————PRACTICE SESSION: EXPLORING——————

Purpose

To give students the opportunity to practice the skill of exploring by using the musical scale model.

Directions

This is to be an in-class practice session. The class will divide into pairs.

Time Needed

Approximately 2 hours

Steps for the Practice

1. The students decide who will take on the role of helper and who will take on the role of client.
2. The student-client shares a problem and the student-helper gives validating responses, stopping after six to eight interchanges.
3. The student-helper writes down what expectations, beliefs, or yearnings she or he hears the student-client carrying.
4. The student-helper shares these with the student-client and they discuss them.
5. The roles are reversed and the process is repeated.
6. The class as a whole discusses the experience.

Identifying Dysfunctional Processes

After exploring and determining where the issues were, Satir would often name the dysfunctional processes she saw.

EXAMPLES WITH AN INDIVIDUAL
"What I'm hearing, Steve, is that you make a promise to yourself and then you don't deliver to yourself. Is that what you are struggling with?"
"So what goes on for you, Maria, is that you think that your husband is too hard on the kids, but you can't tell him. Is that the way it is—that you might get in trouble with him if you did?"

EXAMPLES WITH COUPLES
"What I see happening between the two of you is that you are each feeling pain about what is happening in your relationship, but you show it differently. You, Julio, have become silent and withdrawn. You, Mida, have learned to reach out to the children instead of to Julio. You both want more closeness, but don't know how to make that happen. Does that ring true for each of you?"

"My sense is that the two of you had high hopes for your relationship that
have not come true and that it hasn't been okay to talk about those
disappointments. Is that a possibility?"

EXAMPLES WITH FAMILIES
"One of the things that is coming to me as we talk is that this family
doesn't know how to find out what makes other people happy. Could
that be?"
"As you tell me what a typical day is like in this family, I get the feeling
that people are real hungry for contact, but they don't know how to go
about getting it. Does that seem to fit?"

Educating

Satir believed strongly that people needed new information if they were to
have new choices. She frequently offered information that she felt was needed.
She did this very casually, which seemed to help people accept it.

EXAMPLES WITH INDIVIDUALS
"There are always choices, so let's look at yours in this situation."
"Within us are many wonderful resources, like breathing; so how about
taking a deep breath right now to help settle those butterflies."

EXAMPLES WITH COUPLES
"People can't see their own backsides, so tell your wife how you see her
being with your daughter."
"Communication is to relationships what breath is to life, so let's see if we
can help the two of you talk to each other."

EXAMPLES WITH FAMILIES
"You can go a little closer to your mother, nothing terrible will happen!"
"We learn from our models, so let's take a look at how your parents
parented."

Sculpting

The last skill that will be described in relation to facilitating awareness is
sculpting. Sometimes Satir would use sculpting to share her picture, and
other times to have the client(s) share theirs.

Sculpting to Share Observations

EXAMPLE WITH A COUPLE
"Carl, you stand and face Lila, with one hand on your hip and with the
other hand , point your finger at her and say, 'it's all your fault!' And
Lila, you get down on one knee, put one hand over your heart and the

other reaching up to Carl, and say pathetically, 'Oh, Carl, I'm so sorry, it is all my fault.'"

EXAMPLE WITH A FAMILY

"Juan, you are giving me a picture of how you are experiencing your responsibilities at work and at home. I would like to share that with you. Come, stand up and have all the members of your family hang all over you. . . . Now, is this how it feels to you?"

Sculpting to Elicit Information and Feelings

EXAMPLE WITH A COUPLE

"I think it might be helpful if each of you shared your picture of your relationship. What I would like you to do is show me without using words. Place your partner and yourself in relation to each other the way you experience the relationship. You can be standing, sitting, kneeling, facing toward, facing away, close, distant—whatever will express how you experience the relationship."

EXAMPLE WITH A FAMILY

"I would be very interested in seeing how each of you experience your family. Come, Fred, make a picture of how you see the members of your family relating to each other. Place each person as you see them in relation to the rest."

───── PRACTICE SESSION 1: SCULPTING ─────

Purpose

To give students the opportunity to practice demonstrating the communication stances of placating and blaming.

Directions

This is to be an in-class practice session. Divide into groups of three.

Time Needed

One-half hour

Steps for the Practice

1. Each group chooses a student-helper.
2. The student-helper sculpts the remaining pair, with one student being placed in the blaming stance and the other in the placating stance. It should look like Figure 4.2.
3. The student-helper invites the person in the blaming stance to repeat the phrase "It's all your fault" several times, directed toward

Placating/Blaming

Figure 4.2   Sculpting stances

the person kneeling in the placating position, who then responds by repeating "I'm so sorry; it is all my fault."
4. The student-helper interviews each person about her or his feelings in their exaggerated positions.
5. The student-helper asks the student-clients to resume their normal positions and explores their reactions further.
6. The class reconvenes to discuss the experience.

——— PRACTICE SESSION 2: SCULPTING ———

Purpose

To give the students practice in sculpting.

Directions

This is to be an in-class practice session. Divide into groups of at least five.

Time Needed

Approximately 1 hour per sculpting

Steps for the Practice

1. The students decide who will take on the roles of student-helper and student-client. The three remaining students will participate as role players, taking on the role of the student-client and his or her parents.
2. The student-helper asks the student-client to create a picture of her or his experience with parents or caretakers by placing the role

players in positions that reflect the student-client's perception of the family relationships.

3. The student-helper asks the role players to freeze and hold their positions for about 20 seconds.
4. The student-helper explores with each role player and the student-client the feelings that emerged from the sculpting.
5. The student-helper asks the client to create a new sculpt, depicting any changes she or he would like to make.
6. The student-helper explores with the role players and the student-client feelings that emerge from the new sculpt.
7. The student-helper invites the student-client to become a part of the new sculpting, taking the place of his or her role player and experiencing the new relationships.
8. The student-helper explores the feelings of the student-client.
9. The class reconvenes and discusses the process of sculpting.

Summary of the Beginning Phase

The beginning phase of Satir's process was that of preparing people for making change. This preparation involved making contact and validating people in order to increase their sense of safety and trust. To enhance the depth of her contact with people, Satir used the skills of reaching out, attending, and observing. To help people feel their value, Satir used the skills of engendering hope, affirming, normalizing, appreciating, individualizing, reflecting, clarifying, translating, bridging, and reframing.

Once Satir felt that trust had been established, she would then transition into facilitating greater awareness as to the process issues that were causing the pain and disharmony. Some of the interventions she used for this were mapping, weaving, exploring, identifying dysfunctional processes, educating, and sculpting.

CHAPTER FIVE

The Middle Phase

INVITING INVOLVEMENT AND OWNERSHIP

Contracting

Personalizing

CHALLENGING DYSFUNCTIONAL PATTERNS

Challenging Dysfunctional Behaviors
Challenging Behaviors by Breaking the Rules

Challenging Perceptions

Challenging Interpretations

Challenging Beliefs and Expectations

An Overview of the Middle Phase

In the middle phase, Satir was working to facilitate change by inviting greater involvement and ownership, challenging dysfunctional patterns, and teaching new options. Figure 5.1 lists the skills Satir used to accomplish these goals.

Inviting Involvement and Ownership

Contracting

To involve people more fully in understanding and gaining insight into their behavior and copings, Satir would ask questions that would increase people's desire to be involved and committed to change.

EXAMPLES WITH INDIVIDUALS
"I have a picture of what I think is happening for you. Would you like to hear it?"
"As I hear you speak of your pain, I have some ideas about how you can do something about that. Would you be interested?"

EXAMPLES WITH COUPLES
"I am picking up that you don't know what makes your husband happy. Would you like to hear from him as to what makes him happy?"
"You have been in a blaming place with each other and it hasn't worked. Are you willing to make changes in your way of being with each other?"

EXAMPLES WITH FAMILIES
"I see a picture of what is happening in this family that is causing pain. Do you want to know about my picture?"

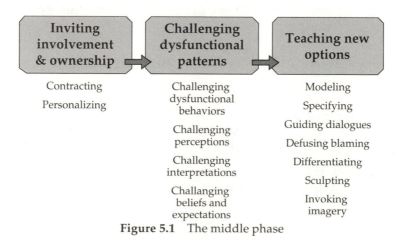

Figure 5.1   The middle phase

"I think people in this family feel misunderstood. I have some ideas about
how this is happening. Would you like to hear them?"

Personalizing

In addition to working to get clients involved in the change process, Satir
would also promote personal responsibility and ownership.[1]

EXAMPLES WITH INDIVIDUALS

"I hear you experiencing the school system as being unfair, and I'm
wondering just what is going on within you that is keeping you from
getting yourself to class."

"As you look to your family to change, I'm wondering how you see
yourself being able to be different with them?"

EXAMPLES WITH COUPLES

"You see your husband as being 'wimpy.' I'm gathering from what you
said earlier that you might know something about that yourself. Is that
true?"

"As you speak, I'm hearing you talk about what you think your wife
wants; but what about you, what do you want, Harry?"

EXAMPLES WITH FAMILIES

"This really doesn't have much to do with your mother, Lynn. It has to do
with you. You know that, don't you?"

"You fear that your children don't know how to stand up for themselves.
Is that true for you as well?"

Challenging Dysfunctional Patterns

Once Satir perceived that clients had achieved involvement and ownership,
she would proceed to challenge any dysfunctional behaviors, perceptions,
beliefs, or expectations.

Challenging Dysfunctional Behaviors

EXAMPLES WITH INDIVIDUALS

"Are you ready to start a new process for yourself?"

"Recognizing that you have a scolding part, would you be open to developing a loving part as well?"

EXAMPLES WITH COUPLES

"Turn toward your partner and let him hear those things you just said to
me."

[1]The skill of Personalizing was identified by Carkhuff & Anthony (1979).

"Let yourself take the risk to believe that your needs matter. Tell your
partner what you need."

EXAMPLES WITH FAMILIES

"As you look at your daughter, are you willing to say to her what is in
your heart?"

"Would you be willing to tell your father what it was like for you when he
left the family?"

Challenging Behaviors by Breaking the Rules

EXAMPLES WITH INDIVIDUALS

"What are you feeling?" (Breaking the rule against feeling.)

"So everyone in your family knew that your father was not faithful to your
mother, but no one talked about it. Is that right?" (Breaking the rule to
keep the family secret.)

EXAMPLES WITH COUPLES

"Would you be willing to risk telling your husband what you want from
him?" (Breaking the rule against asking for what you want.)

"You look as if you have been having strong feelings while your wife was
talking. Can you put words to them?" (Breaking the rule against
expressing.)

EXAMPLES WITH FAMILIES

"What would you like to say to your mother as you see her position in this
sculpting?" (Breaking the rule against expressing.)

"What do you see as you look at this sculpting?" (Breaking the rule against
seeing and expressing.)

Challenging Perceptions

EXAMPLES WITH INDIVIDUALS

"As you focus on your awareness that your father had two siblings who
died from starvation, do you feel any differently about his 'possess-
iveness'?"

"I'm wondering what you know about your parents' courtship. Although
you have a picture of them as unaffectionate, there was a time when
things were different."

EXAMPLES WITH COUPLES

"Mary, as you realize that your husband is not a violent person like your
father was and that your fear belongs to another time, how do you
experience your husband?"

"David, when you see that you react to your partner John so strongly
because of the pain associated with growing-up years, what happens
to your feelings about John?"

EXAMPLES WITH FAMILIES

"Are there times when your partner is loving as well as stubborn?"

"Are you aware that your son is only 8 years old? I hear your worry about him related to your projections of 20 years into the future."

Challenging Interpretations

EXAMPLES WITH INDIVIDUALS

"How is it that you think that you are stupid when you get lower than a superior rating?"

"Your interpretation has been that there is something wrong with you when you don't get a call from your friend. Would you be willing to consider that she may have other distractions that have nothing to do with you?"

EXAMPLES WITH COUPLES

"When your husband sounds angry, you interpret it to mean that he's mad at you. What other possibilities might there be?"

"Your partner says that she meant something very different from what you heard. Are you willing to listen with new ears?"

EXAMPLES WITH FAMILIES

"The meaning you have given to your son moving out is that he is rejecting the family. Based upon his statement here, that he needs his independence but he loves his family, how are you feeling?"

"I'm wondering, how could you be such a bad mother and be here worrying so much about your son's difficulties in school?"

Challenging Beliefs and Expectations

EXAMPLES WITH INDIVIDUALS

"Is it true that you must always be nice? Are there times when it would be okay to be other than nice?"

"Looking at the resources you have just named, is it really true that you have no one to turn to for solace?"

EXAMPLES WITH COUPLES

"Now that you see that you have put an expectation on your spouse that doesn't fit, are you willing to let go of that?"

"Do you really think that if you tell your wife what's going on for you, she will disintegrate?"

EXAMPLES WITH FAMILIES

"As you look at your son, do you really believe that he is the exact replica of your brother who has caused you so much pain?"

"This family appears to me to have a lot of good things going for it. I'm wondering if it's really true that if you are straight with grandma about her need for nursing care, terrible things will happen."

————————PRACTICE————————
HOMEWORK: CHALLENGING

Purpose

To give students practice in identifying dysfunctional beliefs and practice in writing challenges to those beliefs.

Directions

This is to be a homework assignment.

Time Needed

Approximately 1 hour

Steps for the Practice

1. Read the client's statement and identify a possible dysfunctional belief. Then write a challenge, similar to the following example.

CLIENT'S STATEMENT

"I need to lose weight but I can't. I feel safe being overweight."

STUDENT WRITES CHALLENGE

"I'm hearing that you believe that the extra weight keeps you safe and I'm wondering about this. I can imagine someone else believing extra weight to be unsafe. Would you be willing to consider that it's what you say to yourself about being overweight that is really what's creating the sense of safety, not the weight itself?"

The professor then provides feedback to the students about their written responses.

Practice Items

1. Client's statement

    "I am so discouraged about my finances. I am about to lose my house because I haven't been able to pay the mortgage. I don't think it's in the cards for me to have good things happen to me. I've always dreamed of having my own home, but I guess I don't deserve it."

    a.   Write a challenge.

2. Client's statement

    "I am burned out. My nursing job is so demanding that part of me thinks I'm doing enough, but another part thinks I should take on a

second job. There is always this nagging sense that I should be doing more, that it's really not okay for me to do what other people
do. I must do more."

a.   Write a challenge.

3. Client's statement

"I have been having physical symptoms, but the doctor says there's
no physical cause. She said that I should talk to someone about the
stress in my life. I guess I've had a lot of stress, but I didn't think I
needed to talk with anyone about it. I find that difficult to do."

a.   Write a challenge.

——PRACTICE SESSION: CHALLENGING——

Purpose

To give students practice in challenging dysfunction when working
with a couple.

Directions

This is an in-class practice session. Divide into groups of four.

Time Needed

Approximately 1 hour per role play

Steps for the Practice

1 The group begins by deciding who will be the helper, the observer,
   and the two role players. (The role players will take on the roles of a
   couple who are in conflict.)
2. The role-play couple chooses a conflict to work on.
3. The student-helper practices exploring with the couple and challenging any dysfunctional aspects that are elicited.
4. The observer writes down the student-helper's responses.
5. The role play is stopped after approximately 30 minutes, and then
   the observer reads the helper's responses aloud.
6. The student-clients give feedback as to the effectiveness of the
   helper's responses.
7. The class debriefs the experience.

CHAPTER SIX

The Middle Phase Continued

TEACHING NEW OPTIONS

Modeling Congruent Communication

Specifying

Guiding Dialogues

Defusing Blaming

Differentiating

Sculpting

Invoking Imagery

SUMMARY OF THE MIDDLE PHASE

Teaching New Options

Having challenged dysfunctional patterns, Satir offered new options—new possibilities for coping more functionally. Following are some of the ways in which she accomplished this.

Modeling Congruent Communication

Satir used herself as a role model, working to be congruent, clear, specific, direct, and open in her communication with clients.

EXAMPLES WITH INDIVIDUALS

"You know, Myra, I am getting the feeling that something is not right between us. Are there feelings that you are having that you feel unsafe to talk about?"

"What I see, Frank, is that it is very hard for you to let go of the hurt."

EXAMPLES WITH COUPLES

"I see that each of you has inside pain that is coming out in the relationship in hurtful ways."

"So let's get clear here. What would each of you like to have happen in your relationship?"

EXAMPLES WITH FAMILIES

"I'm hearing that Mom's drinking is a problem for this family. Is that true?"

"I believe that even though Dad isn't living with the family now, his presence is being felt very strongly."

Specifying

Satir taught people to be more specific in their language, stating more clearly their meanings, giving more descriptive statements, and so on.

EXAMPLES WITH INDIVIDUALS

"You are saying that you don't see yourself going anywhere. Can you be more specific? What do you mean by 'not going anywhere'?"

"You are encouraged by your progress. What specifically are you doing that is pleasing you?"

EXAMPLES WITH COUPLES

"You are saying that you want more involvement from your husband. What does more involvement mean to you?"

"You don't like the way your wife is looking at you. Tell me what you see."

EXAMPLES WITH FAMILIES

"So you are unhappy with the children's behavior. Tell me, what are the behaviors that are bothering you?"

"What exactly do you want from your husband when it comes to helping out with the discipline?"

Guiding Dialogues

Satir initiated and guided dialogues between people to facilitate better communication. Her guidance included giving directions to clients about where and how to position themselves and how to express themselves.

EXAMPLE WITH A GAY COUPLE

Satir: Joe, can you pull up your chair here a little and turn toward your partner? Talk to him from your heart. Tell him what you are feeling.

Joe: We . . .

Satir: (Interrupting.)   Speak for yourself, Joe; say "I."

Joe: I feel angry that you don't spend more time with me.

Satir: And what else are you feeling? Are you disappointed?

Joe: Yes, I'm disappointed. I thought when you changed jobs, we would have more time together. It seems to me that you don't want to spend time with me.

Satir: Are you saying that you long for being connected with your partner?

Joe: Yes, that's really what I want.

Satir: Tell him that.

Joe: I really want to be more connected with you.

Satir: Jesse, hearing this, how are you feeling?

Jesse: Warm. I didn't know that was what he was feeling. I just saw the anger and got mad.

Satir: Joe, how does it feel having taken the risk to share your heart with Jesse?

Joe: I like the results.

Satir: Wonderful!

EXAMPLE WITH A FAMILY

Satir: Rawanda, I think it might be helpful for your mother to hear what you are thinking and feeling, so just move yourself so you can look at her and tell her.

Rawanda: I don't like the way you hover over me. I can't breathe. You want to know who I'm talking to and about what. You want to know who I'm with, why, and when. Get off my back, mother!

Satir: Rawanda, I'm hearing a lot of pain about this. Tell your mother about the pain.

Rawanda: (Starts to cry.) I don't want to hurt you, mom, but I need space.

Satir: Maya, as you hear your daughter, what feelings come up for you?

Maya: At first, I felt angry and unappreciated; but now that I see her pain, I feel really scared.

Satir: Tell her that.

Maya: I love you. I didn't realize how you were feeling. I want you to have your own life. I'm not sure I can let go by myself, but I am here to get help with that.

Defusing Blaming

One of the most challenging types of dialogue for the therapist to work with is that in which both parties are using a blaming stance. Satir would work to shift the focus off of the "character" of the accused as quickly as possible. She used her creativity to get the direction shifted, sometimes shifting to exploring for facts or history, sometimes asking for behavioral descriptions, and sometimes shifting to process.

EXAMPLE WITH A COUPLE: DIALOGUE 1

Carlita: Chris never listens to me. See how he's ignoring me right now.

Satir: What behaviors do you see that tell you he's not listening? (Shifting the focus to his behaviors and off of Chris's character.)

Carlita: He's looking at the ceiling.

Satir: What else do you see that tells you he's not listening?

Carlita: His facial expression.

Satir: What do you see going on in his face that says to you he's not listening?

Carlita: Well, just the way he's looking.

Satir: What interpretation are you giving to your perception? (Shifting to process by exploring for interpretations.)

Carlita: That he really doesn't want to hear me. That he really doesn't care.

Satir: Okay, that is one possible interpretation. Are you open to any others? (Exploring for openness to new options.)

Carlita: Yes.

Satir:	Chris, tell me, from your perspective, what are you aware of? What was going on with you? (Exploring.)
Chris:	Do you want to know the truth?
Satir:	Yes.
Chris:	I was thinking about a deadline I have at work.
Satir:	Was there any part of you that was feeling upset with Carlita? (Exploring.)
Chris:	I don't think so. I probably wasn't listening. She's right, but it wasn't because I don't care. I do care. I am just preoccupied about this deadline.
Satir:	How are you feeling right now, Carlita? (Exploring.)
Carlita:	Better. I didn't realize that he was so worried about the deadline.

EXAMPLE WITH A COUPLE: DIALOGUE 2

Somaley:	(To husband) You are irresponsible, Sitha. You always make promises and then you don't keep them. You are hopeless!
Satir:	Somaley, I want you to turn toward me and just talk to me right now. Sitha, I will get back to you.
Satir:	Somaley, you sound very disappointed. (Shifting to process, feelings underneath the anger.)
Somaley:	Yes, I am terribly disappointed. I thought Sitha would change, but he's still the same.
Satir:	You had an expectation that he would be different than you are experiencing him to be. (Shifting to expectation.)
Somaley:	Yes, I can't believe he's so irresponsible.
Satir:	What are your feelings at this moment?
Somaley:	Hurt. This isn't the way I wanted it.
Satir:	So you had a picture in your head of how your partner was supposed to be.
Somaley:	I guess so. My dad was irresponsible and I swore to myself that I would never get involved with an irresponsible man.
Satir:	How did it feel when your dad didn't keep his promises?
Somaley:	Terrible. I thought he must not love me.
Satir:	When we are children, we try to make sense out of things. Do you suppose you decided that the reason your dad didn't keep his promise was because you weren't lovable? (Shifting to underlying belief.)
Somaley:	Uh-huh.
Satir:	With your knowledge now as an adult about your dad's struggle with alcoholism, would you be willing to consider that

	when he broke a promise to you, it had to do with him and not with you? (Challenging her belief.)
Somaley:	Yes.
Satir:	How are you feeling right now?" (Reinforcing the change.)
Somaley:	Relief.
Satir:	Would you be willing to turn toward Sitha and look at him, and see if there is anything of your father's that you have put on Sitha? (Exploring for a projection.)
Somaley:	I guess his irresponsibleness.
Satir:	Would you be willing to image your father being beside your husband and see yourself taking the label of "irresponsible" off Sitha and giving it back to your father? (Challenging the projection and teaching a new option.)
Somaley:	Okay, I did it.
Satir:	How are you feeling right now? (Reinforcing the change.)
Somaley:	Good.
Satir:	Okay. Now I would like to check in with Sitha and see what this has been like for him.

As Satir worked with Somaley, she bypassed Somaley's anger and concentrated on her underlying feelings of disappointment and hurt. Satir then led Somaley to an awareness and acceptance of her expectations and beliefs. Once there was acceptance, Satir challenged the belief and helped her let go of it. Finally, Satir shifted the focus back to the present and to Somaley's relationship with her partner, helping her to perceive him more realistically.

Satir then shifted to Sitha, defusing his blaming by eliciting his beliefs and yearnings.

Satir:	Well, Sitha, how has this been for you?
Sitha:	Very interesting. I had no idea that Somaley was putting stuff on me that belonged to her father. She's always nagging me about something! She forgets the things I do right. I can do everything I'm supposed to do for a week and then forget one little thing and she's yelling at me. She's a complete nag!
Satir:	You would like more signs of appreciation. (Shifting to process, stating his yearning.)
Sitha:	Yeah. Wouldn't you? I give up. You can't please women!
Satir:	You have decided that it's impossible to please any woman. (Identifying his belief.)
Sitha:	Well, I haven't been able to please either of my wives and certainly was never able to please my mother. She was on my back all the time. She never gave me credit for anything.

Satir:	Your experience with women has not been good. You have longed for some recognition. (Restating the yearning.)
Sitha:	Sure, who wouldn't?
Satir:	You have yearned for recognition from women for a long time.
Sitha:	Yes, I have.
Satir:	What choices do you see for getting some of that yearning for recognition met with Somaley? (Exploring for new options.)
Sitha:	I don't know.
Satir:	How about asking Somaley if she would be willing to let you know when she appreciates something you have done? I don't know what she will say, but you can ask. (Offering new options.)
Sitha:	Okay.

EXAMPLE WITH A FAMILY: DIALOGUE 1

Lynn:	Jim is too hard on the kids. They commit a misdemeanor, and they get punished for a felony.
Satir:	Now let me see here. Jim is the children's stepfather, is that right? (Shifts focus off accused by exploring history.)
Lynn:	Yes, that's right.
Satir:	And how long have you been married? (Keeping focus off character evaluation.)
Lynn:	Two years.
Satir:	How long was it that you and the children were a unit by yourselves? (Exploring.)
Lynn:	Since Tommy was a year old and Ginny was 3. They are now 14 and 16, so I guess that means we were a unit for 13 years before Jim and I got married.
Satir:	How was that being the only parent for the children? (Shifting the focus onto process.)
Lynn:	Very difficult.
Satir:	How was it difficult for you? (Exploring.)
Lynn:	I got tired of being the disciplinarian.
Satir:	Had you hoped that Jim would come in and take over that task? (Shifting to hopes.)
Jim:	(Interjecting) She sure did! She asked me if I would straighten the kids out. They had gotten out of hand.
Satir:	So it was your understanding that Lynn wanted you to come in and take over? (Reflecting.)
Jim:	Yes, it was.

Satir: Lynn, would you agree that you had expressed a wish that Jim take over? (Personalizing, getting ownership.)

Lynn: Yes, I guess I did. That seems so long ago.

Satir: So what was your expectation of what Jim's parenting would be like? (Shifting to process, exploring for expectation.)

Lynn: Well, I'm not really sure. I just didn't expect him to be so hard on them.

Satir: You're disappointed that it hasn't turned out the way you had hoped? (Reflecting.)

Lynn: Yes, I am. But now I see that I wasn't clear about what I wanted.

Satir: Wonderful. So now, let's have you and Jim talk about this and get clear with each other what you expect. (Reinforcing and teaching new options.)

EXAMPLE WITH A FAMILY: DIALOGUE 2

Sue: Jennifer is being very irresponsible! She knows I have to work and it's her job to take care of the younger ones.

Satir: You are disappointed. (Shifting to process by identifying the feeling under the anger.)

Sue: I sure am. It's hard enough to be the only breadwinner since my husband left, but to have to worry about what's going on at home is just too much.

Satir: You sound as if you feel really burdened. (Reflecting.)

Sue: I really do. I need Jennifer to help me. I know it's a lot to ask of a kid, but I need her.

Satir: I hear you feeling bad for Jennifer, is that right? (Bridging.)

Sue: Yes, I do. I feel really bad. I wish it wasn't this way.

Satir: Well, Jennifer, what is going on with you as you hear your mother? (Bridging.)

Jennifer: I feel better knowing that she can see what it's like for me.

————— PRACTICE HOMEWORK: —————
DEFUSING BLAMING

Purpose

To give students practice in defusing blaming.

Directions

This is to be a homework assignment.

Time Needed

Approximately 2 hours

Step for the Practice

1. Using the preceding dialogues as models, write a dialogue in which two parties are in conflict and are blaming each other, and the helper guides them through the conflict to a nonblaming state.
2. Feedback can be given by the professor.

PRACTICE SESSION: DEFUSING BLAMING

Purpose

To give students practice in defusing blaming.

Directions

This is to be an in-class practice session. Divide into groups of four.

Time Needed

Approximately 1 hour for each role play

Steps for the Practice

1. The group begins by deciding who will be the helper, the observer, and the two clients.
2. The two client role players decide what roles they will take on. They could be partners, parents, a parent and a child, or two siblings. They also decide on their conflict.
3. The student-helper guides them in a dialogue regarding their conflict.
4. The observer notes down as many of the student-helper's responses as possible.
5. The role play is stopped after 30 minutes.
6. The observer reads the student-helper's responses, and the client role players give feedback to the student-helper as to the effectiveness of the responses.
7. The class debriefs the experience.

Differentiating

For Satir, teaching new options included helping people let go of unrealistic expectations. As people were able to let go of expectations of their parents and of themselves, they would be more differentiated, more individuated.

EXAMPLES WITH SELF

"Are you willing to let go of the impossible expectation of yourself that
you should always be there for others?"

"As you feel the pain of expecting yourself to be perfect, are you willing to
let go of that expectation?"

EXAMPLES WITH MOTHER

"Now that you are an adult and have other resources, are you willing to let
go of the expectation that your mother be supportive of you, since she
has not been able to do that? Who would be able to be there for you?"

"After coming to understand your mother's history of rejection, are you
willing to let go of your expectation for her to love you in the way you
want to be loved? How do you see yourself getting that need met in
your life now?"

EXAMPLES WITH FATHER

"Knowing that your father is not able to show you approval in the way
you want it, are you willing to let go of that expectation? You have
other choices now. Where can you look for approval?"

"Understanding now that your father did not receive any nurturing from
his family, is it possible for you to let go of your expectation for him to
nurture you? Who in your current life is capable of nurturing you?"

Sculpting

As described earlier, Satir used sculpting to share her observations and to
learn from others. She also used it to teach people new options. The following dialogue is an example of how she did this.

Satir: Timmy, how about if you create a picture for me of how you
experience your family. Place your mother and your sister as you
experience them, and then put yourself into the picture.

Timmy: Well, my mom would be far away, like over there by the door, and
my sister would be near me pointing her finger and scolding me.

Satir: Okay, now freeze and hold that position. (Waits about 20 seconds
and then tells the participants to relax and share with her what
they experienced.) Now, Timmy, change the picture to the way
you would like it to be.

Timmy: I would bring my mom in and have her between my sister and
me and I would put my sister's finger down.

Satir: Okay, freeze and hold that new position. (Waits again for about
20 seconds.) Now, I would like to hear from each of you as to
how you felt in your new position. Let's start with Timmy.

It should be noted that sometimes students focus rather exclusively on the intervention of sculpting, ignoring the other intervention possibilities. Although sculpting can be very useful, it is limiting without the full range of other intervention choices.

————PRACTICE SESSION: SCULPTING————

Purpose

To give students practice in sculpting.

Directions

This is be an in-class practice session for the whole class.

Time Needed

Approximately 1 hour for each sculpting

Steps for the Practice

1. The group decides who will take on the roles of client and helper.
2. The student-client selects role players to play the members of her or his real family of origin, including a stand-in for her- or himself.
3. The student-helper directs the student-client to picture the relationships in her or his family and to position the role players accordingly.
4. The helper directs the group to freeze and hold their positions. (Student-helper waits 20 seconds.)
5. The helper tells the group to relax and interviews them as to what each felt in their respective positions.
6. The helper directs the client to make changes in the sculpt as to the way she or he would have liked it to be.
7. The helper directs the role players to freeze and hold their new positions.
8. The helper directs them to relax and interviews them about their experience in their new positions.
9. The helper interviews the client as to how she or he is feeling after hearing from the role players.
10. The class discusses the experience.

Invoking Imagery

Satir used imagery as another means of creating change. She often used it to explore the images that were being held and then to propel the process forward by eliciting or offering new possibilities through imagery.

EXAMPLE WITH AN INDIVIDUAL

Satir: Hue, what picture do you see as you talk to me about your fear of your mother?

Hue: I see us on the boat after the war and my mother being very angry.

Satir: Does she behave in that manner now?

Hue: No.

Satir: So when you fear your mother now, you are really reacting to an earlier picture.

Hue: Yes, I guess I am.

Satir: As you see your mother on the boat, looking back with adult eyes, what do see?

Hue: I see someone who was terrified for herself and her children.

Satir: And as you have that awareness, how do you feel?

Hue: More relaxed. It's helpful to picture my mother as frightened rather than angry.

EXAMPLE WITH A COUPLE

Satir: Latonya, when you say that you don't trust what DeJohn tells you, you have a lot of energy behind the words. I'm wondering if you have any images that come up for you around the word "trust." You might even want to close your eyes to connect with them.

Latonya: The picture I'm getting is of when I was 5 and my dad left us. He and my mom had a very bad argument and he left. I never saw him again until I was 25 years old.

Satir: And what feelings are there for you as you see that scene again?

Latonya: (Weeping.) Sadness, terrible sadness. I lost my daddy that day.

Satir: That was extremely painful.

Latonya: Yes. I think these tears have been in me ever since.

Satir: Are you feeling a release as they flow out of you?

Latonya: Uh-huh. It was so painful. Our lives were never the same after that. I guess that's the reason it is so hard for me to trust DeJohn. I have such a fear that one day he'll walk out of my life like my dad did.

Satir: So your experience with your dad is spilling over to DeJohn?

Latonya: Yes. I don't want that anymore. It makes things miserable between us.

Satir: What images could you bring to mind that might help you with this? How can you separate out your present from your past?

Latonya: I'm not sure. I feel so much better already just having been able to cry. I guess what I'm experiencing is seeing my dad when he used to play with me. No longer is the image of him walking out the door my only image.

Satir: Wonderful. (Touches Latonya's arm.)

EXAMPLE WITH A FAMILY

Satir: Carlos, as I hear you speak of your pain about the difference between your son's attitude about money and your own, I sense a lot of energy with this. What pictures come to mind as you think about growing up in Mexico?

Carlos: I see horrible poverty. We had no money. My uncle who was already in the United States would send us money from his job as a cook sometimes. My parents would be desperate for the money. He would send us money and in the envelope there would be one stick of Juicy Fruit gum. You can't imagine how precious that stick of gum was to us kids. We would divide it up and each treasure our little tiny piece. And now my son thinks nothing of buying a $15 CD! It makes me furious!

Satir: When you reconnect with your suffering as a child, you have pain and rage for what you experienced. You would have liked some of the comforts you have been able to provide for your son.

Carlos: Yes. I sure would have. I would have been grateful for a tenth of what he's gotten. . . . But I guess that's not his fault. He doesn't have any way to understand how difficult it was for me in Mexico.

Summary of the Middle Phase

In the middle phase of Satir's therapeutic process, she used many different skills to facilitate change, frequently starting by attempting to gain greater involvement and ownership through such skills as contracting and personalizing. This increased involvement set the stage for taking people into the heart of her therapeutic process: that of challenging dysfunctionality and teaching new options regarding attitudes and behaviors.

With individuals, challenging dysfunctionality meant working at the various levels of the Self, such as challenging dysfunctional perceptions, expectations, or beliefs. With couples and families, challenging dysfunctionality meant challenging dysfunctional patterns of communication.

After challenging an individual's internal process or a couple's or family's interactional process, Satir would teach them new options by such interventions as modeling, guiding dialogues, defusing blaming, differentiating, sculpting, and imagery.

CHAPTER SEVEN

The End Phase

GUIDING PRACTICE

Coaching

Imagery Rehearsal

HIGHLIGHTING POSITIVE CHANGES

Affirming Changes

Emphasizing

Anchoring

SUMMARY OF THE END PHASE

An Overview of the End Phase

In the end phase of a helping interaction, Satir worked to reinforce the positive changes that had been made. She often did this by guiding people in practicing new ways of being, which could take the form of actually coaching people as they practiced new behaviors or guiding them in an imagery rehearsal process.

Satir also reinforced positive changes by her words and tone. At times, she would use her words and tone to reinforce by affirming people's resources and capacities. Other times, she would emphasize a positive change by calling attention to it. Still other times, Satir would reinforce a change by anchoring it—asking people how they felt after a change had been made. The skills used in the end phase are outlined in Figure 7.1.

Guiding Practice

Coaching

Satir coached people in the practice of new behaviors to help them become familiar with these behaviors and truly integrate them.

EXAMPLES WITH INDIVIDUALS
"Now that you have put your dreams out to me, Paul, how about practicing putting them out to your father? Just imagine him here and let the words come out of your throat."
"Having taken the step to tell me one of your wants, I'd like to invite you to practice this new skill by telling me another."

EXAMPLES WITH COUPLES
"Tony, turn toward your partner and tell him what you are telling me."
"How about telling your partner even more things that you appreciate about her, Tyrone?"

EXAMPLES WITH FAMILIES
"Now that this family is aware of being able to be straight with each other, how about practicing this in relation to the issue of the will that has

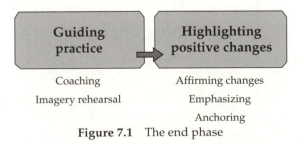

Figure 7.1   The end phase

just been brought up? Fumiko, you start. Say straight how you feel about the issue of the will."

"And now that you parents have expressed your appreciation to me regarding the efforts your children have made this week, how about saying them directly and specifically to the children?"

Imagery Rehearsal

Satir used imagery to reinforce new behaviors by asking people to close their eyes and imagine future situations in which they could use their newly acquired behaviors.

EXAMPLES WITH INDIVIDUALS
"Would you be willing to close your eyes and see yourself talking to yourself in this new, kinder way the next time you make a mistake?"
"Can you close your eyes and practice seeing yourself connected with your courage as you begin to take the steps you want to take?"

EXAMPLES WITH COUPLES
"Having just experienced being straight and clear in your communication with each other here, would you be willing to close your eyes and see yourself doing this at home?"
"I'm wondering if the two of you would be willng to close your eyes and see yourself being in this new way with each other the next time you encounter a difference."

EXAMPLES WITH FAMILIES
"Can you just close your eyes and breathe and imagine yourself staying this centered as you talk with your mother-in-law?"
"How about if each of you in this family close your eyes and picture yourself continuing to be this straight with each other as you leave here and go on with your lives?"

Highlighting Positive Changes

Satir reinforced changes by highlighting them. Following are some of the skills she used for highlighting positive changes.

Affirming Changes

Satir would notice a positive attribute or change and point it out.

EXAMPLES WITH INDIVIDUALS
"Did you know that you could have that much impact on someone?"
"I just heard you put out a want of yours. You have wants, too!"

EXAMPLES WITH COUPLES

"Are you aware of the wonderful interaction that just took place between the two of you?"

"And now the two of you know you have the ability to talk with each other about the special things that are in your heart."

EXAMPLES WITH FAMILIES

"I'm aware that this family is now at a place where people can share things straight and be honored for that. Are you all aware of that?"

"You all just took your courage in hand and talked about your differences. Did you know you had that kind of courage?"

Emphasizing

Satir would make positive comments, emphasizing her support for change. Her comments were often accompanied with a loving touch as well.

EXAMPLES WITH INDIVIDUALS

"I'm so glad you were able to get those things out that have been stuck inside."

"Oh, that's wonderful that you could tell me that!"

EXAMPLES WITH COUPLES

"Okay, that's good that you could get that straight with each other."

"How wonderful that you two can now be with each other in this new way!"

EXAMPLES WITH FAMILIES

"It's marvelous that you could say this to your parents. Now they have new information for understanding you."

"I can see very positive things happening as this family begins to talk with each other in different ways."

Anchoring

Satir also reinforced changes by underscoring significant changes in perceptions, feelings, beliefs, or behaviors.

EXAMPLES WITH INDIVIDUALS

"How do you feel having shared this with me?"

"Now that you can see the steps toward your goal, how does that feel?"

EXAMPLES WITH COUPLES

"Be with that new feeling of expressing your feelings to your husband."

"How does it feel to have shared your wants with your wife?"

EXAMPLES WITH FAMILIES

"Just be in this new place with your son for a moment."

"Seeing these new possibilities for your family, how do you feel at this
  moment?"

──────PRACTICE SESSION: COACHING────── AND REINFORCING NEW BEHAVIORS

Purpose

> To give students experience in coaching and reinforcing.

Directions

> This is to be an in-class practice session. Divide into triads.

Time Needed

> Approximately 1 hour per role play

Steps for the Practice

1. Each group begins by deciding who will take the roles of helper,
   client, and observer.
2. The student-client presents a problem to the student-helper.
3. The student-helper attempts to take the student-client through all
   the phases, including practicing and reinforcing a new behavior.
   (Keep in mind, however, that the primary responsibility of a
   therapist is to be respectful of the client's process, so if it does not
   seem appropriate to proceed to behavioral practice, do not do so.)
4. The observer records the helper's responses and reads them aloud
   afterward.
5. The group discusses the effectiveness of each response as it is read.
6. The students change roles and repeat the process.
7. The class discusses the experience.

Summary of the End Phase

Because Satir believed practice to be the last stage of the change process, she
uusally incorporated practice into the ending phase of her work. She would
do this in different ways, sometimes in directing dialogues, coaching people
in new ways of communicating, and sometimes through imagery rehearsal.

In additional to guiding people in practicing new behaviors, Satir reinforced positive changes by using such skills as affirming, emphasizing, and
anchoring.

PRACTICE HOMEWORK: USING SKILLS FROM ALL PHASES

Purpose

To give students the opportunity to practice using skills from all three phases.

Directions

This is to be a homework assignment.

Time Needed

Approximately 2 hours

Steps for the Practice

1. Imagine that you are the therapist for your own family of origin, and write an assessment of your family, identifying the strengths that will be reinforced and the areas of dysfunction that need to be addressed. Then the professor can provide you with feedback. Here is an example with a student named Lupe and her parents, Jose and Maria.

   a. Strengths

   My parents came from Mexico and they have endured many hardships. My family is very supportive in times of crisis. My family is hardworking.

   b. Areas needing attention

   My parents both have low self-esteem. My father uses blaming as a primary communication style and my mother uses placating. I have been placed in a parentified child role with inappropriate expectations for me in terms of my responsibilities toward my siblings. There is a covert rule that we don't talk about feelings.

2. On the basis of the assessment, each student writes a treatment plan for her or his family of origin, which includes specific interventions for each phase, along with examples of how the intervention would be applied. Here is a short example.

   a. Beginning phase: Lupe writes

   I would make contact, observe, and validate the members of my family while mapping out our family history for the past three generations. This would give me rich material to highlight my parents' capacity for enduring pain and hardship. Specific interventions I could use are affirming, engendering hope, and weaving. These are some examples.

Affirming: "Jose, are you aware of how much courage and capacity to endure you have?"

Engendering hope: "I can see this capacity serving you well as we work together."

Weaving: "Now, that we have looked at the grandparents' ways of coping, let's look at yours, Jose and Maria."

b. Middle phase: Lupe writes

I would work on helping my parents communicate in more congruent ways, which would include talking about feelings. And I would work on modifying my parents' expectations of my responsibilities. Specific interventions I could use are activating dialogues and breaking the rules.

Activating a dialogue: "Jose and Maria, I would like for you to turn toward each other. Maria, would you be willing to tell Jose how you feel about the amount of overtime he works and what you would like instead?"

Breaking the rules: "Lupe, would you share with your parents what it is like for you to carry many of the parenting responsibilities?"

c. End phase: Lupe writes

I would reinforce changes through positive comments as the members of my family were able to share honest feelings. Specific interventions I could use are emphasizing and anchoring.

Emphasizing: "How wonderful, Maria, to see you stating your desires!"

Anchoring: "Lupe, how does it feel to be able to share your feelings with your parents?"

———————PRACTICE SESSION:———————
USING SKILLS FROM ALL PHASES

Purpose

To give students the opportunity to practice using skills from all three phases.

Directions

This is to be an in-class practice session. Divide into groups of at least seven.

Time Needed

Approximately 2 hours per role play

Steps for the Practice

1. The students begin by deciding who will practice being the helper and who will be the observers of the helper. It is helpful to use two observers, if possible.
2. The rest of the students become a role-play family. Two students take on parent roles, with the remainder being the children.
3. The role-play family separates from the helper and decides on the following:
    a. *Their presenting problem:* An acting-out teen, a younger child with behavioral problems, stepfamily conflicts, marital problems, or substance abuse
    b. *The communication stances of the parents:* Blaming, placating, being super-reasonable, or distracting
    c. *The role of each child:* Peacemaker, parental messenger, family clown, family hero, mom's or dad's ally, surrogate spouse, scapegoat, or the lost child
4. The student-helper conducts a family session for 30 minutes, starting with making contact and validating, and then moving into making changes and reinforcing those changes.
5. The observers write down the helper's responses verbatim and stop the session after 30 minutes.
6. After the session, the observers read the helper's responses, and the group attempts to identify the responses that were the most helpful.
7. The class reconvenes and discusses the experience.

CHAPTER EIGHT

Satir's Therapeutic Process Illustrated

TRANSCRIPTION OF A SESSION WITH SATIR

Transcription of a Session with Satir

The script from the videotape *Forgiving Parents* has been transcribed so readers can study Satir's process as she takes the client through all the phases and uses many of the skills described in the text.* In this session, Satir is working at a workshop with a woman named Linda, who holds resentments toward her mother for having been and still being extremely critical of her. Linda has asked Satir for help in dealing with her mother's criticism. Linda describes her mother as criticizing her because she is too thin, talks too loudly, and doesn't make good use of her musical talent. When this example begins, Satir is asking Linda to consider a different response to her mother's criticism.

Satir: Linda, can you thank your mother for noticing you? Then say to her, "Mother, I've been meaning to share with you that I know you've often noticed my weight, and I would like to tell you how I feel about my body." (Guiding and modeling.) Say the noticing part first, then how you feel about your body. I think your mother worries that you are going to die. (Reframing.) You are not thanking her for criticizing you, but for noticing you. (Educating.) "What does that feel like?" (Exploring feelings.)

Linda: I'm confused. When do I say what you are telling me and when do I say that I don't want to hear that I am too skinny anymore?

Satir: Well, saying "thanks for noticing" is the first step. What do you have to do to help yourself to do that? (Guiding, exploring, and specifying.)

Linda: It seems like I have to shift my perceptions from seeing my mother's criticism as a way of putting me down to a way of showing me love.

Satir: Well, it might be loving. I don't know about that for sure, but I think there is some of that. I don't want to push anything down your throat. I can see you still feel rejected and vulnerable. (Reflecting feelings, thereby validating.)

Linda: Yes.

Satir: (Asks Linda to choose someone from the group to role-play her mother.) Ask your mother if she ever loved and valued you. (Guiding.)

Linda: Have you ever loved and valued me?

Mother: (Role player.) Yes. I had dreams for you. You were going to be what I couldn't be.

Satir: Do you believe that, Linda? (Exploring beliefs.)

---

*The dialogue is taken from the film "Forgiving Parents," produced by NLP Comprehensive and printed in *The Patterns of Her Magic,* by Steve Andreas, Science and Behavior Books, Los Altos, CA.

Linda: Uh-huh.

Satir: Come closer, just a step closer to your mother, while you let yourself believe that. (Guiding and reinforcing.)

Satir: What was your mother's life like as a child? (Exploring perception.)

Linda: Very hard. Her father was abusive to her.

Satir: So your mother had a lot of training about how she was bad and not okay? (Educating and reframing.)

Linda: Yes.

Satir: I know you know a lot about that too. (Bridging.) Look at your mother now. (Guiding.) What are you feeling? (Exploring feelings.)

Linda: Love and sadness.

Satir: Just be with that for a moment. (Anchoring.)

Linda: If I were to say everything that I have wanted to say to my mother, both wonderful and painful, it would unleash a lot of emotion for her.

Satir: She would cry. All that happens when people cry is that they get tears. I've never seen any building explode! (Challenging a catastrophic expectation.) So now look at your mother and talk to her about the things that are wonderful and things that are painful. (Guiding.) Because you know, Linda, this is about you, not your mother. You know that don't you? (Personalizing.)

Linda: Yes.

Satir: Okay. (Reinforcing.)

Satir: So as you look at your mother, what is that like for you?" (Exploring feelings.)

Linda: Scary.

Satir: That's because it's new. (Educating.) Are the odds enough for you to risk doing something you have never done before?

Linda: I've asked myself that a lot. I feel like I am working on my relationship with my mother already by practicing new ways of interacting with other women.

Satir: That's not the same. Those women are not your mother. (Challenging.) What are you feeling right now? (Exploring.)

Linda: I'm afraid of coming out of hiding with my mother.

Satir: I'm hearing your yearning that you want to be loved and valued. (Identifying the yearning.) But a piece of you says, "Be careful about who you get to love and value you." Is that true? (Creating awareness of her defense.)

Linda: Uh-huh.

Satir: So you have your caution in front of you. Could you consider having your caution beside you, instead of in front of you? (Guiding.) Can you go inside yourself and know your mother as a human being and know that the way she is had very little to do with you. Do you know that? (Educating.)

Linda: Yes.

Satir: But the hurt has gone on for so many years and you are still leaving it all up to your mother. (Personalizing.) What about you starting a new process? (Challenging.) Can you recognize that as an adult you have learned new things that you didn't know as a child? Your mother wouldn't know how to do this. (Educating.) Could you show her the way? (Contracting.)

Linda: I'd like to.

Satir: Look at her (mother role player) and let that be what you are in touch with. (Guiding.) What does that feel like? (Exploring feelings.)

Linda: I'm willing. I've been looking for a way.

Satir: Okay, now I'd like for you to say, "Thank you for paying attention to me, and there are some things in the way you pay attention to me that don't fit for me." (Guiding.) Go up to her and take her hand as you thank her because that is what she needs. (Educating.) So that you can say, "You know, I've been worried about my weight, too. I can't seem to gain." (Modeling and guiding.) Can you imagine yourself doing that now? (Guiding.)

Linda: Yes.

Satir: Let's see what happens as you move it out of your throat. (Guiding.)

Linda: Mother, thank you for noticing me, but I need to tell you that. . . .

Satir: Leave the "but" off. Let it be a complete sentence by itself. (Guiding.)

Linda: Mother, I really appreciate you noticing me. The thing with the weight has come up so often. I see that you are worried about me and I suggest that you not worry because I'm healthy.

Satir: Just be in touch with how it feels to be sharing this delicate truthful part of yourself with your mother in a context of acknowledging her presence as well. (Anchoring.)

Linda: It feels schizophrenic. One part feels good and another part is scared.

Satir: Well, the last thing I want is for you to feel you have to do anything different, but if something in you wants to move out in some way or another, then that's okay, too. (Validating.)

Linda: I'm feeling fear, trying to let go and transform to love.

Satir: Give me a picture of your fear. (Invoking imagery.)

Linda: Opening up communication with my mother so that we say things to each other that would be hurting.

Satir: Okay, I think I'm getting a sense of this. In your quest to get a new connection with your mother, your fear is, and it might be justified, that you will make things worse. Is that it? (Reflecting and clarifying in order to validate.)

Linda: Yes.

Satir: Are you aware that you really don't have this to say to your mother, but to your image of your mother? (Challenging interpretation.)

Linda: Intellectually, but I can't seem to bring that through.

Satir: Here is a pillow that represents your image of your mother. Tell the pillow all of your angers. (Guiding.)

Linda: I want to tell her . . .

Satir: Say "you" to her. (Guiding.)

Linda: You really hurt me, not being able to ever nurture me, even bathe me.

Satir: Close your eyes and go inside and see if it's really true that you never got a bath. (Challenging.)

Linda: Well, maybe sometimes . . . but why couldn't she nurture me? I was a wonderful little baby.

Satir: Where did you get that idea? (Exploring belief.)

Linda: I just know I was!

Satir: Open your eyes and look at me and see that wonderful part. (Anchoring.) Your mother knew that, too. (Educating.)

Linda: I know that she did, but she didn't put it out.

Satir: How long are you going to keep troubling yourself for somebody who had it on the inside but couldn't put it out?" (Challenging and personalizing.)

Linda: I'm looking. I'd like to end it right now.

Satir: Is there any part of you that doesn't believe she cared about you? (Exploring belief.)

Linda: Part of her loved me beyond belief and part of her wanted to destroy me.

Satir: What part loved you? (Exploring.)

Linda: Her heart.

Satir: And what part wanted to destroy you? (Exploring.)

Linda: Her upbringing.

Satir: This is brilliant. You know what was stopping your mother from expressing what was in her heart. (Reinforcing.)

Satir: Pick out role players from the group to come up and be your mother's family. Place them in relation to each other, showing how it was to be in her family. (Sculpting.)

Linda: Sculpts her mother's father kicking her mother with the children cowering in front of their abusive father.

Satir: Shame comes to me so strongly as I look at your mother's family. I can hear your mother saying to you, "What a shame that you aren't doing more with your music!" (Educating as to the origins of the mother's critical behavior.)

Satir: Now this scene gives us a feel for your mother's experience as a child. If we go forward in time, how did your father come on the scene to get together with your mother? (Mapping.)

Linda: He was funny and he sang. He was attracted to my mother because she was moral, Catholic, and religious.

Satir: Okay, so he didn't expect her to fool around. Were the women on his side kind of loose? (Mapping.)

Linda: No. His parents both died when he was very young, and he was raised by his older brother and his brother's wife.

Satir: Was his brother's wife loose? (Exploring.)

Linda: No.

Satir: Well, someone was loose in this family, I can tell you that! (Educating.)

Linda: My father was! He was a wild and crazy kind of guy.

Satir: Okay, so I want you to think about how people are. Your father is wild and loose and your mother looks like she's full of integrity. Can you imagine that he saw your mother's integrity as a support for him? And she would depend on him to bring light into her life! (Educating.)

Satir: (To Linda's role-play father:) "Go into her mother's family here on stage and rescue her from this family and sing while you do it!" (Guiding.) Role-player father goes into the sculpted mother's family and takes the role-play mother out of the sculpt to a separate part of the stage where they act out singing and having fun together.

Satir: Now, as you look at your parents, what are you feeling? (Exploring feelings.)

Linda: They are cute.

Satir: Just be with that. (Anchoring new perception.)

Satir: What your father didn't know about your mother is that her rigidity would be over everything, way beyond her integrity. (Educating.) What your mother didn't know about your father is that his funniness would go against her sense of order. So what was used as a way to get together became a yoke around their necks. (Educating and reframing.)

Satir: Let's bring your brothers and sisters up on stage. How many brothers and sisters did you have? (Mapping.)

Linda: I had one older brother and a younger sister.

Satir: Okay, choose role players from the group to be your brother and sister and place them as you experienced them in relation to your parents. Also choose someone to stand in for you in the family. (Sculpting.)

Linda: My brother would be distanced from the family with his back turned and his head bowed.

Satir: What happened to your brother? (Mapping.)

Linda: He's an alcoholic.

Satir: Yes, he would have to do something like that. Being an alcoholic doesn't mean he wasn't bright or nice. It just means when the pain was too great, he drank to numb himself. (Educating and reframing.)

Satir: What about your sister? (Mapping.)

Linda: She ran away, became a mother, then ran away from her child, then became a hippie, and now she's a "born-again Christian."

Satir: Okay. What did you do?

Linda: I hung in there and tried to make everybody happy.

Satir: Did you succeed even a little bit? (Exploring.)

Linda: Oh, yeah.

Satir: Just be with that. How does that feel? (Exploring feelings.)

Linda: It's a burden.

Satir: Okay, role players, I would like for you to take your postures real tight and make sounds and movements that fit your position. (Sculpting.) And now role players, I'd like for you to give yourself a message of appreciation and take a deep breath, letting your body expand to meet the breath until you are standing on your own two feet and free to move. Now when you get on your own feet, look around and do what you want. (Family role players hug each other.)

Satir: As you watched, Linda, what did you see happen? (Exploring.)

Linda: Fear transformed into love.

Satir: Look at your mother. She tried hard, but she wasn't all that successful. As you look at her now, what are you aware of feeling? (Exploring feelings.)

Linda: A lot more compassion.

Satir: Can you move a little closer and see what that feels like?" (Guiding and challenging her to change.) Linda spontaneously moves all the way over to her and hugs her.

Satir: Be aware that you are now touching the life force of your mother. What you experienced before were the behaviors of your mother because the life force didn't have a place to express itself. (Anchoring, educating, and reframing.)

Satir: (To Linda, after Linda stopped hugging her mother:) How was that for you? (Anchoring.)

Linda: I don't know if I can put it into words. It was very helpful. I have desperately wanted to talk to my mother differently, but I was missing the connection for how to do it.

Satir: Can you see yourself doing it in the future? (Imagery rehearsal.) You have a different expression on your face and in your eyes, which tells me that you have moved to a different place in yourself. (Anchoring.) I don't know what your transactions with your mother will be, but I do know you'll never look at your mother in the same way again. She will never look at you in the same way because you will come in with something different. (Anchoring and educating.)

Linda: I feel something has shifted and I think you're right, I won't be able to look at my mother in the same way again. I feel clearer and more loving. Thank you very much for this, Virginia. It was wonderful for me!

Selected Family Therapy Outcomes: Bowen, Haley, and Satir

In 1993, Winter published the results of a large-scale research project, conducted in the 1980s by the Family Institute of Virginia, that assessed the effects of the models of Satir, Haley, and Bowen. The study evaluated the effectiveness of family therapy with youths involved in the juvenile justice system of the State of Virginia and their families ($n = 249$). Each juvenile's family was assigned to one of four groups, three of which were treatment groups—one for each clinical approach ($n = 188$)—and one of which was a compari-

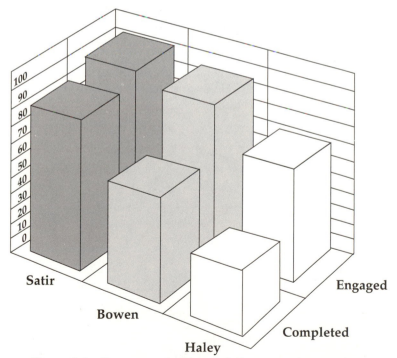

Figure A.1 Engagement and completion percentages among Bowen theory, strategic family therapy, and the Satir process model

son group ($n = 61$). The comparison group received the normal court services but not family therapy.

The psychotherapy outcome variables of engagement, dropout, completion, locus of control, family functioning, satisfaction with therapist, and satisfaction with outcome were evaluated. The results revealed that with regard to the variables of engagement, dropout, and completion, Satir's process model both engaged and retained a significantly higher proportion of families in therapy, demonstrating a greater rate of treatment retention and completion than either the Bowen or Haley clinical approaches.

Examination of the "Locus of Control" variable—the variable measuring an individual's perception of events as the result of one's own behavior (internal), as opposed to either the result of luck, fate, or chance (external)—found that all three treatment groups had moved toward being more internally oriented.

The subscales measuring the variables of adaptability and family cohesion, however, revealed no significant changes in relation to mothers, fathers, and identified clients, with one exception: the identified clients in the Satir and Haley treatment groups demonstrated a significant increase on the cohesion subscale.

With regard to the variable satisfaction with treatment outcome, Winter summarized her findings, stating that "family members in the Bowen and Haley samples were significantly less satisfied with treatment than those in the Satir group. Further, identified clients in the Satir sample reached a higher level of satisfaction with treatment outcome than those in the Bowen and Haley groups (Winter, 1993, p. 585).

Similarly, for the variable satisfaction with therapist, the Satir model ranked highest, followed by the Haley and Bowen groups (Winter, 1993, pp. 555–587).

Family Making: A Multifamily Therapy Research Project

On-going research which assesses the effectiveness of Satir's theory and practice with parolee families in a residential recovery program is being conducted by Dr. Sharon Armstrong and Gregory Armstrong. The research is sponsored by the Association for Marriage and Family Therapy Research and Education Foundation and Avanta, The Satir Network. Initial research began in 1996 and involved both a control group and a treatment group. The treatment group consisted of 20 families who participated in the project called "Family Making" (Armstrong & Armstrong, 1997). The treatment modality consisted of multifamily treatment groups meeting for one intensive weekend workshop, with follow-up groups. Pre- and posttests were administered to both the treatment group and the control group, to assess for changes in family cohesion, family conflict, self-esteem, marital satisfaction and symptoms of depression.

Preliminary data are not adequate for establishing statistical significance, but they do suggest the efficacy of the "Family Making" program for improving family cohesion and reducing conflict. On the Family Environment Scale, family cohesion increased an average of 21% with a reduction in conflict of 11%. The measures of self-esteem and depression showed slight improvement. Because only three participants were in a relationship, the measure of marital satisfaction was dropped from the study. There was inadequate control group data due to unforeseen factors; therefore, additional follow-up research with another comparison group will be conducted. The recidivism rates of the parolees in the study are being tracked and analyzed and may be published in a future study.

Effects of the Satir Model on African-American Family Caregivers

In 1994, research assessing the effectiveness of the "Self-Directed Skills Nursing Model" was conducted by Catherine Caston at the University of Iowa for her doctoral dissertation. The model was based on the Satir paradigm and involved African-American primary family caregivers who were caring for a frail, homebound relative. The focus of the study was to determine the effect of Satir's model on self-esteem, health service utilization, enmeshment, burden, and burnout of the family caregivers. A total of 60 caregivers were used in the study—30 experimental and 30 control—with both qualitative and quantitative analysis of the data.

The results indicated that the primary family caregivers' self-esteem, burden, and burnout scores were statistically significant. The global rating indicated high enmeshment preintervention, and low enmeshment postintervention. Health service utilization did not increase pre- or postintervention. The findings also suggested that coping patterns of African-American primary family caregivers in the home is costly, both physically and emotionally (Caston, 1994).

Answers to Practice Assignments

Practice Homework: Validating Skills

1. Response (b) was chosen because it attempts to clarify the meaning of the client's message, whereas (a) focuses on the content of the client's sharing.
2. Response (b) was chosen because it attempts to clarify the client's feeling, whereas response (a) takes the focus away from the client's message.
3. Response (b) was chosen because it is an attempt to reflect the feeling and meaning of the client's message, whereas response (a) is shifting the focus toward the client's behavior.
4. Response (a) was chosen because it focuses on trying to understand the client's feelings toward his girlfriend, whereas response (b) gives advice.
5. Response (a) was chosen because it brings out the underlying message, whereas response (b) is a statement of the helper's opinion.
6. Response (a) was chosen because it goes to the underlying feeling, whereas response (b) is a statement of opinion.

Practice Homework 1: Shifting to Process

1. (a) Intrapersonal—the therapist is exploring the internal process of the mother
   (b) Interpersonal—the therapist is exploring the parents' communication process
   (c) Triangular—the therapist is questioning the mother about the interaction of two of her children
   (d) Systemic—the therapist is asking about the process of the family as a whole
2. (a) Interpersonal—the therapist is exploring about the interaction possibilities of the mother and daughter

(b) Triangular—the therapist is asking the daughter to describe her parents' interaction

(c) Intrapersonal—the therapist is exploring the internal process of the adult daughter

(d) Systemic—the therapist is asking about the entire family and its process regarding risking being vulnerable and stating needs

Practice Homework 2: Shifting to Process

1. Response (b) was selected because the focus was shifted away from the content—the mother's moving—and onto the client's internal process.
2. Response (a) was selected because the focus was shifted from the content of the husband's behaviors onto the couple's process regarding dealing with differences.
3. Response (b) was selected because it shifted from the content of the children's behavior onto the mother's family's process in relation to showing respect.

Practice Homework 1: Exploring

1. Dialogue 1
   a. that if people aren't calling, they don't want her for a friend
      that she is not likable
      that she can't keep friends
      that she is defective
2. Dialogue 2
   a. that he is not really valued
      that he is not worthy of being in the group
      that he can never do enough
      that he will be rejected
      that it's not okay to say "no"
      that he will always be on the outside
3. Dialogue 3
   a. that his efforts are not appreciated
      that women cannot be satisfied
      that he will never be understood
      that violence is the only way to get his needs met
      that others are responsible for his behavior
      that if he has a feeling, he must act on it
4. Dialogue 4
   a. that she must placate others and sacrifice herself in order to prevent abandonment

that it's not okay to ask for help
that it's not okay to express wants and needs
that she can't function without her husband
that she is not worth being respected

References

Armstrong, S., & Armstrong, G. (1997). *Family making: A multifamily therapy research project*. Unpublished raw data.

Branden, N. (1994). *The six pillars of self-esteem*. New York: Bantam.

Carkhuff, R. R. & Anthony, W. A. (1979). *The skills of helping: An introduction to counseling*. Amherst, MA: Human Resource Development Press.

Caston, Catherine. (1994). *Self-directed skills nursing model: Decrease burnout in African-American caregivers*. The University of Iowa, Iowa City, IA.

Foley, V. D. (1974). *An introduction to family therapy*. New York: Grune & Stratton.

Goldenberg, I., & Goldenberg, H. (1991). *Family therapy, an overview*. Pacific Grove, CA: Brooks/Cole.

Kramer, S. (1995). *Transforming the inner and outer family*. New York: Haworth Press.

Loeschen, S. (1991). *The secrets of Satir*. Desert Hot Springs, CA: Event Horizon Press.

Nerin, W. (1986). *Family reconstruction: A long day's journey into light*. New York: Norton.

Nichols, M., & Schwartz, R. (1995). *Family therapy*. Boston: Allyn & Bacon.

"Remembering Virginia." (1988, Jan/Feb.). *The Family Networker*. Silver Spring, MD.

Russell, D. (1986). *A conversation with Virginia Satir, Virginia Satir Collection*. Santa Barbara, CA: Humanistic Psychology Archive.

Satir, V. (1978). *Your many faces*. Palo Alto, CA: Science and Behavior Books.

Satir, V. (1983). *Conjoint family therapy*. Palo Alto, CA: Science and Behavior Books.

Satir, V. (1988). *The new peoplemaking*. Palo Alto, CA: Science and Behavior Books.

Satir, V., & Baldwin, M. (1983). *Satir step by step: A guide to creating change in families*. Palo Alto, CA: Science and Behavior Books.

Satir, V., & Baldwin, M. (1987). *The use of self*. New York: Haworth Press.

Satir, V., Bandler, R., & Grinder, J. (1976). *Changing with families*. Palo Alto, CA: Science and Behavior Books.

Satir, V., Banmen, J., Gerber, J., & Gomori, M. (1991). *The Satir model.* Palo Alto, CA: Science and Behavior Books.

Satir, V., & Englander-Golden. (1990). *Say it straight.* Palo Alto, CA: Science and Behavior Books.

Schwab, J. (1983). *The use of Satir concepts in field instruction.* Unpublished manuscript.

Schwab, J. (1990). *A resource handbook for Satir concepts.* Palo Alto, CA: Science and Behavior Books.

Schwartz, R. (1995). *Internal family systems.* New York: Guilford Press.

Sprenkle, D., Keeney, B., & Sutton, P. (1982). Theorists who influence clinical members of AAMFT: A research note. *Journal of Marital and Family Therapy, 8,* 367–369.

Winter, J. (1993). *Selected family therapy outcomes with Bowen, Haley, and Satir.* Ann Arbor, MI: University Microfilms International.

Videotapes

Satir, V. (1985). *Of rocks and flowers: Dealing with the abuse of children.* Kansas City, MO: Golden Triad Films.

Satir, V. (1989). *Self-worth.* Boulder, CO: NLP Comprehensive.

Satir, V. (1990). *Forgiving parents.* Boulder, CO: NLP Comprehensive.

Satir, V. (1992a). *Communication stances.* Issaquah, WA: Avanta: The Virginia Satir Network.

Satir, V. (1992b). *The origins and transformations of survival copings.* Issaquah, WA: Avanta: The Virginia Satir Network.

Satir, V. (1992c). *The process of change.* Issaquah, WA: Avanta: The Virginia Satir Network.

Satir, V. (1992d). *The seed model.* Issaquah, WA: Avanta: The Virginia Satir Network.

Index